I0152040

PRAYING WITH JESUS

A Journey Through the Lord's Prayer

Daniel Hall

Real Fast Publications

Copyright © 2025 Daniel Hall

All rights reserved

No part of this book may be reproduced, or stored in a retrieval system, or transmitted in any form or by any means, electronic, mechanical, photocopying, recording, or otherwise, without express written permission of the publisher.

Ebook Edition: ISBN: 978-0-943941-24-0
Paperback Edition: ISBN: 978-0-943941-26-4

For business inquiries please contact Daniel Hall @
daniel@danielhallbonus.com
Printed in the United States of America

To all who seek.

CONTENTS

INTRODUCTION

The Lord's Prayer is remarkably concise - just 65 words in its most familiar form, taking less than 30 seconds to recite. Yet within this brief prayer lies an extraordinary depth of wisdom that continues to resonate through our daily lives.

I've always been struck by how this simple prayer manages to address the full spectrum of human experience. From acknowledging our spiritual connection to seeking daily provision, from processing guilt to finding strength against temptation - it's all there, distilled into a few powerful lines that countless people across history have found transformative.

What fascinates me is how practical the Lord's Prayer remains in our modern context. When we feel overwhelmed by life's complexities, these timeless words offer clarity. When we struggle with forgiveness, they remind us of its importance. When we face difficult decisions, they provide a moral compass. When anxiety threatens to consume us, they offer a path to surrender and peace.

Throughout this book, we'll explore how this ancient prayer speaks directly to our contemporary challenges, offering wisdom that's both profoundly simple and simply profound. The Lord's Prayer isn't just a religious text to be recited - it's a practical guide for living, as relevant in today's world as it was when first spoken two thousand years ago.

~ Daniel Hall

CHAPTER 1: THE LORD'S PRAYER IN CONTEXT

Historical Setting of the Lord's Prayer

The Lord's Prayer emerges from a complex and turbulent period in history - first-century Palestine under Roman occupation. This era was marked by political tension, social upheaval, and religious fervor, all of which profoundly influenced the context in which Jesus taught this transformative prayer.

At the time, Palestine was firmly under the control of the Roman Empire. The Jewish people, once rulers of their own kingdom, now found themselves subjects of a foreign power. This occupation brought with it a host of challenges: heavy taxation, the presence of Roman soldiers, and the imposition of Roman cultural norms. The tension between Jewish religious practices and Roman imperial rule created a backdrop of constant conflict and messianic expectation.

This political climate fueled an intense period of messianic anticipation among the Jewish population. Many Jews eagerly awaited a divine intervention that would restore their nation's autonomy and usher in God's kingdom on earth. This hope for a messiah - a divinely appointed leader who would overthrow the Romans and reestablish Jewish sovereignty - colored much of the religious and political discourse of the time.

Within this charged atmosphere, various Jewish religious movements sought to interpret and respond to their circumstances. The Pharisees, known for their strict adherence to the law and oral traditions, gained significant influence among the common people. The Sadducees, often aligned with the wealthy elite, held sway in the Temple and were more accommodating to Roman rule. The Essenes withdrew from mainstream society, forming isolated communities dedicated to purity and preparation for the end times. The Zealots advocated for armed rebellion against Rome, viewing violent resistance as a religious duty.

Beyond the specifically Jewish context, the wider Greco-Roman world exerted considerable influence on the culture of Palestine. The Greek language, introduced centuries earlier during the Hellenistic period, remained a lingua franca for trade and scholarly discourse. Greek philosophy and Roman governance models shaped intellectual and political thought, creating a complex cultural landscape where traditional Jewish beliefs interacted with foreign concepts.

Amidst these religious and political currents, the daily realities of life for most people in Palestine were often harsh. Many struggled with poverty, exacerbated by heavy taxation from both Roman authorities and the Temple system. Social inequality was stark, with a small elite holding most of the wealth and power. For the average person, concerns about "daily bread" were far from metaphorical - they reflected the very real challenges of securing sustenance in a difficult economic environment.

It was into this multifaceted world that Jesus introduced the Lord's Prayer. Its simplicity and directness stood in contrast to the complex religious and political debates of the day. Yet, each phrase of the prayer resonated deeply with the hopes, fears, and daily struggles of those who first heard it. The prayer's call for

God's kingdom to come echoed the messianic longings of the time. Its request for daily bread spoke to the economic hardships faced by many. Its emphasis on forgiveness addressed the need for social healing in a fractured society.

Understanding this historical context enriches our appreciation of the Lord's Prayer. It reveals how Jesus, deeply attuned to the realities of his time, offered a prayer that was both profoundly relevant to its immediate setting and timelessly applicable to future generations. The prayer provided a spiritual compass for navigating the complexities of life under Roman rule, while also transcending its specific historical moment to offer guidance for all who seek connection with God.

Biblical Context of the Lord's Prayer

The Lord's Prayer holds a significant place within the biblical narrative, appearing in two distinct Gospel accounts. In Matthew's Gospel, the prayer is presented as part of Jesus' broader teaching during the Sermon on the Mount. Here, it serves as a model for righteous living and authentic spirituality, contrasting with the ostentatious prayers of some religious leaders of the time. Matthew's account places the prayer within a larger discourse on how to live out one's faith in a manner pleasing to God.

Luke's Gospel, on the other hand, introduces the Lord's Prayer in a different context. In Luke's narrative, Jesus offers this prayer in response to his disciples' specific request for guidance on how to pray. This setting emphasizes the prayer's role as a practical tool for spiritual communication, given directly from teacher to students.

The contrast between Jesus' teaching on prayer and the contemporary prayer practices of his time is striking. While some religious leaders of the day were known for their lengthy, public prayers designed to impress onlookers, Jesus advocated for simplicity and sincerity in approaching God. The Lord's

Prayer, in its concise yet comprehensive form, embodies this principle of meaningful, unpretentious communication with the Divine.

Despite its revolutionary aspects, the Lord's Prayer is not disconnected from the rich tradition of Jewish prayer. Elements of the prayer echo passages from the Psalms and prophetic writings, grounding it firmly in the soil of Jewish spiritual practice. For instance, the concept of God as Father, while given new depth in Jesus' teaching, has roots in Old Testament scripture. Similarly, the emphasis on God's kingdom and will being done on earth as in heaven resonates with prophetic visions of divine rule.

The Lord's Prayer also aligns seamlessly with Jesus' broader teachings on prayer and spirituality. Throughout the Gospels, Jesus emphasizes the importance of seeking God's kingdom first, trusting in divine provision, and maintaining a forgiving spirit. These themes are central to the Lord's Prayer, making it a concise summary of Jesus' overall message about relating to God and others.

In both Gospel accounts, the prayer serves as more than just a set of words to recite. It provides a framework for understanding the nature of God, the human condition, and the relationship between the two. By teaching his followers to address God as Father, Jesus invites them into a intimate, trusting relationship with the Divine. At the same time, the prayer's petitions for daily bread, forgiveness, and deliverance from evil acknowledge human dependency and vulnerability.

The placement of the Lord's Prayer within the biblical narrative also highlights its role in shaping Christian identity. As part of Jesus' core teachings, the prayer became a fundamental element of early Christian practice and belief. It served not only as a guide for personal prayer but also as a communal declaration of faith and allegiance to God's kingdom.

In essence, the biblical context of the Lord's Prayer reveals its multifaceted nature. It is at once a practical guide for prayer, a theological statement, a summary of Jesus' teachings, and a charter for Christian living. Its presence in the Gospels ensures its central place in Christian spirituality, while its connection to Jewish tradition bridges the Old and New Testaments. As we continue to study this prayer, its rich biblical context will inform our understanding of its individual components and overall significance.

Theological Significance of the Lord's Prayer

The Lord's Prayer, despite its brevity, carries profound theological weight that has shaped Christian understanding of God, humanity, and the nature of spiritual life for centuries. At its core, this prayer introduces and reinforces several revolutionary concepts that were radical in Jesus' time and continue to challenge and inspire believers today.

Perhaps the most striking theological innovation in the Lord's Prayer is the concept of addressing God as "Father." In the cultural context of first-century Judaism, this intimate form of address was largely unprecedented. By encouraging his followers to approach God with the familiar term "Abba," Jesus introduced a radical shift in how humans could relate to the divine. This concept of God as a loving, approachable father figure was a departure from the more distant, awe-inspiring depiction of God common in many Jewish prayers of the time. The implications of this shift are profound, suggesting a relationship with God based on love, trust, and intimacy rather than fear or mere obligation.

However, the prayer doesn't solely emphasize God's nearness. It masterfully balances the concept of divine immanence with that of transcendence. While God is addressed as Father, He is also acknowledged as being "in heaven." This tension between God's intimate accessibility and His ultimate otherness creates a theological framework that respects both the closeness of God to human experience and the vast gulf between divine and human nature. It invites believers into a relationship with God that is simultaneously intimate and reverent.

Central to the theology of the Lord's Prayer is the concept of God's kingdom. The petition "Thy kingdom come" encapsulates a core theme of Jesus' ministry and early Christian belief. This kingdom theology presents a vision of God's rule being established on earth, suggesting a transformation of current realities to align with divine will. It implies that the present world order is not final and that God's followers should actively participate in bringing about this new reality.

The prayer also addresses the theological concepts of human dependency and divine provision. By instructing his followers to ask for "daily bread," Jesus acknowledges the ongoing nature of human need and the corresponding constancy of God's care. This simple request carries deep implications about the nature of human existence – we are not self-sufficient, but continually reliant on God's generosity. It fosters an attitude of humility and gratitude, countering tendencies toward pride or self-reliance.

Finally, the Lord's Prayer doesn't shy away from the realities of human moral struggles and spiritual warfare. By including petitions for forgiveness and protection from temptation and evil, it presents a theology that is deeply aware of human frailty and the ongoing battle between good and evil. The prayer acknowledges the reality of sin while simultaneously affirming the possibility of forgiveness, creating a framework for understanding human moral responsibility and divine grace.

The reciprocal nature of forgiveness presented in the prayer – "forgive us our debts, as we forgive our debtors" – introduces a challenging ethical dimension to this theology. It suggests that human participation in the cycle of forgiveness is integral to experiencing divine forgiveness, linking vertical (God-human) and horizontal (human-human) relationships in a profound way.

In essence, the theological significance of the Lord's Prayer lies in its ability to distill complex theological concepts into a brief, accessible form. It presents a God who is both transcendent and immanent, a vision of divine rule breaking into human reality, an acknowledgment of human dependency and frailty, and a call to participate in the divine attributes of provision and forgiveness. This theological richness, contained in such a concise prayer, has provided fertile ground for reflection, debate, and spiritual growth throughout Christian history.

Cultural Impact and Universal Appeal

The Lord's Prayer has transcended its origins in first-century Palestine to become a cornerstone of Christian worship and a significant cultural touchstone worldwide. Its influence extends far beyond the confines of religious practice, permeating literature, art, language, and even secular discourse.

One of the most remarkable aspects of the Lord's Prayer is its widespread use across Christian denominations. Despite the doctrinal differences that often divide various Christian traditions, this prayer serves as a unifying element. Whether in a Roman Catholic mass, an Eastern Orthodox liturgy, or a Protestant service, the Lord's Prayer is likely to be heard, providing a shared spiritual language for Christians around the globe. This universal adoption speaks to the prayer's ability to capture essential Christian beliefs and practices in a concise, memorable form.

The impact of the Lord's Prayer on Western culture and language cannot be overstated. Phrases from the prayer have become deeply embedded in common parlance, often used even by those unfamiliar with their religious origins. Expressions like "daily bread," "lead us not into temptation," and "thy will be done" have found their way into literature, music, and everyday speech. The prayer's influence can be seen in works ranging from

Dante's "Divine Comedy" to Tolkien's "The Lord of the Rings," demonstrating its enduring power as a source of inspiration and reflection.

As Christianity spread globally, the Lord's Prayer became one of the most translated texts in history. From ancient Syriac to modern Swahili, the prayer has been rendered in countless languages, often serving as a tool for linguistic preservation. In many cases, the translation of the Lord's Prayer into a local language has been a crucial step in the development of written forms for previously unwritten languages. This process has not only aided in the spread of Christianity but has also contributed significantly to linguistic and cultural preservation efforts worldwide.

Interestingly, the Lord's Prayer has garnered attention and respect even beyond Christian circles. Some Jewish scholars recognize the prayer's roots in Jewish tradition, particularly its similarities to the Kaddish prayer. Islamic perspectives often appreciate its monotheistic emphasis and its focus on submission to God's will. This interfaith appreciation highlights the prayer's ability to speak to universal human experiences and aspirations.

Even in secular and philosophical contexts, the Lord's Prayer has been a subject of analysis and admiration. Ethicists and moral philosophers have found value in the prayer's ethical framework, particularly its emphasis on forgiveness, communal welfare, and the rejection of materialism. The prayer's balance between individual needs and collective concerns provides a model for ethical reflection that transcends religious boundaries.

The adaptations and interpretations of the Lord's Prayer across different cultures reveal its remarkable flexibility. While the core elements remain consistent, the prayer has been contextualized in myriad ways. In some cultures, "daily bread" might be rendered as "daily rice" or another staple food. In others, the concept of "debt" as sin might be expressed through culturally specific metaphors. These adaptations demonstrate the prayer's ability to speak to diverse human experiences while maintaining its essential message.

The Lord's Prayer's cultural impact is also evident in its use in times of crisis or national significance. It has been recited at presidential inaugurations, in times of war, and during natural disasters, serving as a source of comfort and unity even in largely secular contexts. This widespread use underscores the prayer's ability to provide solace and express shared hopes and fears, even for those who may not fully embrace its religious implications.

In conclusion, the cultural impact and universal appeal of the Lord's Prayer extend far beyond its religious origins. Its influence on language, literature, and ethical thought, its adaptability across cultures, and its ability to unite diverse groups of people all testify to its enduring power. As both a religious text and a cultural artifact, the Lord's Prayer continues to shape how people around the world conceptualize their relationship with the divine, their ethical obligations, and their place in the human community.

Structure and Composition of the Lord's Prayer

The Lord's Prayer, despite its brevity, exhibits a remarkable depth in its structure and composition. This carefully crafted prayer serves as a model of spiritual communication, balancing various elements of praise, petition, and ethical commitment.

At its core, the prayer follows a thoughtful organization that guides the supplicant through a comprehensive approach to communion with God. It begins with praise and acknowledgment of God's sovereignty, moves to petitions for both spiritual and material needs, and concludes with ethical obligations and a recognition of human dependence on divine grace. This structure provides a template for believers, teaching them to approach God with reverence, express their needs, and commit to living according to divine principles.

One of the most striking features of the Lord's Prayer is its ability to balance spiritual and material concerns. By including both transcendent requests like "thy kingdom come" and practical needs such as "our daily bread," the prayer acknowledges the full spectrum of human needs and aspirations. This balance reflects a holistic understanding of human existence, recognizing that spiritual growth and physical well-being are intertwined aspects of life.

The prayer employs literary devices such as parallelism and repetition to enhance its impact and memorability. The repeated use of "thy" in the first half and "us" in the second creates a rhythmic structure that not only aids in memorization but also emphasizes key themes. This parallelism subtly reinforces the relationship between God's will and human needs, suggesting that alignment with divine purposes leads to the fulfillment of human necessities.

Perhaps one of the most remarkable aspects of the Lord's Prayer is its conciseness and memorability. In just a few short lines, it encapsulates core Christian beliefs and practices. This efficiency in conveying complex theological ideas makes it accessible to believers of all backgrounds and educational levels. Its brevity allows for frequent recitation, enabling the prayer to become deeply ingrained in the hearts and minds of those who use it regularly.

Despite its concise nature, the prayer demonstrates a remarkable adaptability for both personal and communal use. While employing plural pronouns like "our" and "us," suggesting a communal context, the content of the prayer is equally applicable to individual devotion. This dual functionality allows the prayer to serve as a unifying element in corporate worship while also providing a framework for personal spiritual reflection.

The structure of the Lord's Prayer also reflects a progression from the heavenly to the earthly, from God's glory to human need. It begins with a focus on God's name, kingdom, and will before turning to human needs for provision, forgiveness, and protection. This arrangement teaches supplicants to prioritize God's purposes over personal desires, aligning human will with divine intention.

In conclusion, the structure and composition of the Lord's Prayer reveal a carefully designed template for spiritual communication. Its balanced content, memorable format, and adaptable nature have contributed to its enduring impact across centuries and cultures. As we continue to study and recite this prayer, we gain deeper insights into its artful construction and the profound wisdom it contains.

The Lord's Prayer in Early Christian Tradition

The Lord's Prayer quickly became a cornerstone of early Christian practice and thought, shaping the faith and identity of believers in the centuries following Jesus' ministry. Its influence extended far beyond its original context, becoming a unifying force in Christian worship, education, and theology.

In the early Church, the Lord's Prayer played a crucial role in catechesis and baptismal preparation. As new converts sought to join the Christian community, they were instructed in the essentials of the faith, with the Lord's Prayer serving as a foundational text. Its concise yet comprehensive nature made it an ideal summary of Christian beliefs and practices. Catechumens were often required to memorize and recite the prayer as part of their preparation for baptism, demonstrating their understanding of and commitment to the Christian way of life.

The incorporation of the Lord's Prayer into Christian liturgy occurred relatively early in Church history. By the second century, it had become a standard element in many Christian worship services, often recited just before the celebration of communion. This placement emphasized the prayer's themes of unity, forgiveness, and dependence on God, which were seen as essential preparations for partaking in the Eucharist. The regular communal recitation of the prayer helped to reinforce Christian identity and foster a sense of unity among believers.

Early Church Fathers devoted considerable attention to interpreting and expounding upon the Lord's Prayer. Tertullian, writing in the late second century, famously referred to it as the "epitome of the whole Gospel," recognizing how it encapsulated core Christian teachings in a concise form. Augustine of Hippo wrote extensively on the prayer, offering detailed theological reflections on each petition. These patristic commentaries not only deepened understanding of the prayer but also used it as a launching point for broader theological discussions on topics such as the nature of God, the kingdom, sin, and spiritual warfare.

The textual transmission of the Lord's Prayer reveals interesting variations in early manuscripts. Most notably, the doxology "For thine is the kingdom, and the power, and the glory, forever. Amen" appears in some later manuscripts but is absent from the earliest known texts. This variation led to differences in usage among Christian traditions, with some incorporating the doxology into their recitation of the prayer and others omitting it. These textual issues sparked scholarly debates and theological reflections on the nature of scripture and tradition.

Perhaps most significantly, the Lord's Prayer played a crucial role in shaping Christian identity in the early centuries of the Church. Regular recitation of the prayer became a marker of Christian belonging, distinguishing believers from other religious groups. Its use in both public worship and private devotion helped to create a shared language of faith that transcended geographical and cultural boundaries. The prayer's emphasis on addressing God as Father, seeking His kingdom, and living in forgiveness and dependence on divine provision articulated a distinctively Christian worldview.

The Lord's Prayer also served as a tool for spiritual formation in the early Church. Its petitions were seen as a guide for aligning one's desires and actions with God's will. Early Christian writers encouraged believers to not merely recite the words but to internalize their meaning, allowing the prayer to shape their thoughts, attitudes, and behaviors.

As Christianity spread throughout the Roman Empire and beyond, the Lord's Prayer was translated into numerous languages, often serving as one of the first texts rendered in a new tongue. This process of translation not only aided in the spread of Christianity but also contributed to the preservation and development of many languages.

The centrality of the Lord's Prayer in early Christian tradition set the stage for its enduring influence throughout Church history. Its role in worship, education, and personal devotion established patterns that would persist for centuries, shaping Christian spirituality and theology in profound ways. The early Church's engagement with this prayer bequeathed to subsequent generations a rich heritage of reflection and practice, inviting each new era of believers to encounter afresh the timeless wisdom encapsulated in Jesus' teaching on prayer.

Contemporary Relevance and Challenges

The Lord's Prayer, despite its ancient origins, continues to resonate deeply in our modern world, addressing contemporary spiritual needs while also presenting new challenges for interpretation and application.

In an age characterized by anxiety, materialism, and rapid technological change, the prayer's emphasis on trust, contentment, and spiritual priorities offers a countercultural perspective. Its call to seek first the kingdom of God provides a grounding force for those overwhelmed by the constant demands of modern life. The simple request for "daily bread" serves as a powerful reminder to cultivate gratitude and to resist the endless pursuit of material excess that often defines contemporary consumer culture.

The prayer has also emerged as a vital tool in ecumenical and interfaith dialogue. Its universal themes of forgiveness, ethical living, and the pursuit of divine guidance provide common ground for discussions between different Christian denominations and even across faith traditions. Many find that the prayer's core principles align with values shared by various religious and philosophical systems, making it a bridge for understanding and cooperation in our increasingly diverse global society.

However, the prayer's ancient text has sparked ongoing linguistic and translation debates. Scholars and religious leaders continue to grapple with how best to render phrases like "daily bread" and "lead us not into temptation" in modern languages, seeking to balance fidelity to the original text with clarity for contemporary audiences. These debates often reflect deeper theological discussions about the nature of God, human free will, and the role of divine intervention in daily life.

Interestingly, the psychological and social impact of the Lord's Prayer has become a subject of scientific study. Research has shown that regular recitation of the prayer can have measurable effects on individual well-being, reducing anxiety and fostering a sense of connection with others. Some studies suggest that the prayer's structure and content activate areas of the brain associated with empathy and social cognition, potentially explaining its enduring power to create a sense of community among those who pray it together.

Despite its enduring popularity, the Lord's Prayer faces challenges to its relevance and interpretation in the modern world. Some critics argue that its language and concepts are too rooted in ancient patriarchal and hierarchical worldviews to speak effectively to contemporary issues. In response, some modern theologians have proposed alternative versions that address concerns like environmental stewardship, social justice, or gender inclusivity.

For example, some communities have experimented with phrases like "Our Father-Mother in heaven" or added lines about caring for the earth. Others have sought to reinterpret traditional phrases through a modern lens, seeing "daily bread" as encompassing not just physical sustenance but also emotional and spiritual nourishment in a complex world.

These reinterpretations and adaptations reflect an ongoing tension between preserving the prayer's traditional form and ensuring its continued relevance. They also demonstrate the prayer's remarkable adaptability, as each generation finds new depths of meaning in its ancient words.

Ultimately, the contemporary relevance of the Lord's Prayer lies in its ability to address timeless human needs - for guidance, forgiveness, provision, and protection - while also providing a framework for engaging with the unique challenges of our time. As we continue to grapple with issues of faith, ethics, and human flourishing in a rapidly changing world, this ancient prayer offers both comfort and challenge, inviting us to align our lives with its vision of a world transformed by divine love and human cooperation.

CHAPTER 2: "OUR FATHER": INTIMACY AND REVERENCE IN ADDRESSING GOD

The Revolutionary Concept of God as Father

In the rich tapestry of religious history, few concepts have been as transformative as Jesus' invitation to address God as "Father." This idea, central to the Lord's Prayer, marked a significant departure from the prevailing Jewish understanding of God in the Old Testament.

Throughout the Old Testament, God was primarily portrayed as a transcendent, powerful, and sometimes fearsome deity. The Israelites' encounter with God at Mount Sinai, as described in Exodus 19:16-19, exemplifies this perspective. The people trembled at the foot of the mountain, overwhelmed by thunder, lightning, and the sound of a loud trumpet, as God descended in fire and smoke. This awe-inspiring and often intimidating image of God was deeply ingrained in Jewish consciousness.

Enter Jesus, whose unique relationship with the Father fundamentally reshaped this understanding. Throughout His ministry, Jesus consistently referred to God as His Father and, remarkably, invited His followers to do the same. This intimate connection was not just a theological concept for Jesus; it was a lived reality. We see this in moments like Mark 14:36, where Jesus, in the Garden of Gethsemane, addresses God as "Abba, Father." This personal, intimate form of address was unprecedented in Jewish prayer tradition.

The term "Abba" itself carries profound significance. This Aramaic word, which Jesus would have used in His daily life, is more than just a formal title. It's an intimate term, similar to "Daddy" in English, yet maintaining an underlying tone of respect. By using and encouraging this form of address, Jesus was introducing a radical new way of relating to God – one characterized by closeness and familial love, rather than distant reverence alone.

This shift in addressing God was nothing short of revolutionary. In the context of first-century Judaism, where God's name was considered too holy to even pronounce, the idea of addressing the Almighty as one would address a loving father was shocking. Religious leaders of the time would have found this approach bordering on blasphemous. Yet, Jesus not only used this form of address Himself but taught His disciples to do the same, as we see in the Lord's Prayer.

The implications of this concept for believers' identity cannot be overstated. Recognizing God as Father elevates the status of believers from mere creatures or servants to beloved children. As 1 John 3:1 beautifully expresses, "See what great love the Father has lavished on us, that we should be called children of God!" This new identity brings with it a sense of belonging, security, and intimate access to God that was previously unimaginable.

This revolutionary concept of God as Father doesn't diminish God's majesty or power. Instead, it adds a profound dimension of love and intimacy to our understanding of the divine. It invites us into a relationship where we can approach the throne of grace with confidence, knowing that we are addressing not just the Creator of the universe, but our loving Father.

As we continue to explore the Lord's Prayer, this foundational understanding of God as our Father will shape how we approach each subsequent phrase. It sets the stage for a prayer life and a faith journey characterized by both intimate trust and deep reverence, forever changing how we relate to the Divine.

Balancing Intimacy and Reverence

In our journey to understand the profound implications of addressing God as "Our Father," we must navigate the delicate balance between intimacy and reverence. This balance is crucial for developing a mature and meaningful relationship with God.

The concept of God as Father, while revolutionary and deeply personal, can sometimes lead to an overly casual approach to the Divine. There's a danger in viewing God solely as a "buddy" figure, losing sight of His majesty and holiness. Some modern worship songs, for instance, have been criticized for lacking reverence, treating God like a casual friend rather than the Creator of the universe. While God desires closeness with His children, He is still the Almighty, deserving of our utmost respect and awe.

Maintaining reverence is crucial in our relationship with God. The prophet Isaiah's vision in Isaiah 6 vividly demonstrates the awe-inspiring nature of God's holiness. In this passage, even the seraphim cover their faces in God's presence, crying out, "Holy, holy, holy is the Lord Almighty." This serves as a powerful reminder that while God invites us into an intimate relationship, He remains the transcendent, all-powerful deity.

The phrase "who art in heaven" that follows "Our Father" in the Lord's Prayer serves as a reverence qualifier. It reminds us that while God is our Father, He is also the sovereign ruler of the universe. This phrase beautifully balances the intimate address with a recognition of God's transcendence, helping us maintain a proper perspective in our approach to Him.

Throughout scripture, we find examples of this delicate balance between intimacy and reverence. In Psalm 42, for instance, the psalmist longs for God with the intimacy of a deer panting for water, while simultaneously acknowledging God's majesty as the living God. This psalm exemplifies how deep personal longing can coexist with profound reverence.

Practically cultivating both intimacy and reverence in our prayer life requires intentionality. One approach is to start prayers with adoration and acknowledgment of God's holiness before moving into personal requests. This practice helps set the tone for our conversation with God, reminding us of who we're addressing.

Another practical step is to incorporate moments of silent reflection or even physical postures of reverence, such as kneeling or bowing, into our prayer time. These physical acts can help align our hearts and minds with the reverence due to God.

It's also beneficial to regularly meditate on scriptures that highlight both God's intimate love and His transcendent majesty. The book of Revelation, for example, provides powerful imagery of God's throne room, which can instill a sense of awe, while the Gospels show Jesus' tender interactions with individuals, fostering a sense of God's personal care.

In our daily lives, we can cultivate reverence by practicing the presence of God – being mindful of His constant presence in every situation. This awareness can help us approach life decisions, interactions with others, and even our private thoughts with a sense of being in God's holy presence.

Balancing intimacy and reverence in our relationship with God is not about rigid rules, but about cultivating a heart attitude that recognizes both God's incredible love for us and His unmatched holiness. As we grow in this balance, we'll find our relationship with our Heavenly Father deepening, becoming both more intimate and more profoundly respectful.

By maintaining this balance, we can fully embrace the privilege of calling God our Father while never losing sight of His majesty. This approach to our relationship with God will inform not just our prayer life, but how we live out our faith in every aspect of our lives, leading to a richer, more mature spiritual journey.

The Communal Aspect of "Our Father"

When Jesus taught His disciples to pray "Our Father," He was introducing a revolutionary concept that extended far beyond individual spirituality. The use of the plural pronoun "Our" instead of "My" carries profound implications for how we understand our relationship with God and with each other.

The significance of using "Our" rather than "My" cannot be overstated. Even in our most private moments of prayer, we are reminded that we are part of a larger family of believers. This simple word choice emphasizes that our spiritual journey is not meant to be solitary, but rather a shared experience with our brothers and sisters in faith. It challenges us to think beyond our personal needs and desires, considering the collective needs of God's family.

This communal aspect of addressing God as "Our Father" aligns perfectly with the New Testament teaching on believers as adopted children of God. The Apostle Paul, in his letter to the Galatians, beautifully illustrates this concept: "But when the fullness of time had come, God sent forth his Son, born of woman, born under the law, to redeem those who were under the law, so that we might receive adoption as sons" (Galatians 4:4-5). This adoption into God's family is not an individual event but a collective one, uniting all believers under the fatherhood of God.

The implications of this shared divine fatherhood for church unity are profound. When we truly internalize the concept of

God as "Our Father," it becomes a powerful force for breaking down barriers within the church. Differences in race, class, nationality, or social status pale in comparison to our shared identity as children of God. This understanding should compel us to treat our fellow believers with the love and respect due to family members, fostering a spirit of unity and mutual care within the church.

Moreover, this concept of shared fatherhood extends beyond the walls of the church, influencing our social responsibility and ethics. If we truly believe that all people are potential children of God, it should radically alter how we treat others, especially those who are marginalized or different from us. The parable of the Good Samaritan takes on new depth when we consider that the injured man on the road is not just a stranger, but potentially a brother in God's family.

However, it's important to note that while the Lord's Prayer emphasizes the communal aspect of faith, it doesn't negate the personal nature of our relationship with God. There's a delicate balance to be struck between individual faith and community involvement. Salvation is indeed a personal matter – each individual must make their own decision to follow Christ. Yet, the Lord's Prayer reminds us that this personal faith is lived out in the context of community.

This tension between the individual and communal aspects of faith reflects the broader Christian understanding of the church as both a gathering of individuals and a unified body. We are called to nurture our personal relationship with God while simultaneously recognizing our place within the larger family of believers.

In practical terms, this understanding of God as "Our Father" should influence how we approach church life and Christian community. It calls us to move beyond mere attendance or casual association to deep, familial relationships with our fellow believers. It challenges us to care for one another as true brothers and sisters, sharing in each other's joys and sorrows, and supporting one another in our spiritual journeys.

Ultimately, the use of "Our Father" in the Lord's Prayer is a powerful reminder that in Christ, we are never alone. We are part of a vast, diverse, yet united family under the fatherhood of God. As we pray these words, may we be ever mindful of our place within this divine family, and may it shape how we relate to God, to our fellow believers, and to the world around us.

Theological Implications of God as Father

The concept of God as Father carries profound theological implications that shape our understanding of the divine nature and our relationship with God. This idea is intricately linked to the doctrine of the Trinity, where God is revealed as Father, Son, and Holy Spirit. The Father's relationship with Jesus, the eternal Son, forms the basis for our understanding of divine fatherhood. When we address God as Father in prayer, we're not just using a metaphor, but participating in the very life of the Trinity. The Holy Spirit enables us to cry "Abba, Father," as Paul writes in Romans 8:15, allowing us to share in Jesus' intimate relationship with the Father.

However, this concept has not been without challenges. Feminist theologians and others have critiqued the use of exclusively male language for God, arguing that it reinforces patriarchal structures and limits our understanding of the divine. Some advocate for more inclusive language, suggesting terms like "Parent" or incorporating feminine imagery for God. Others maintain that the biblical revelation of God as Father is essential and shouldn't be altered. This debate highlights the tension between honoring biblical tradition and addressing contemporary concerns about gender and representation in religious language.

The concept of God as a loving Father also intersects with the perennial problem of evil and suffering. How can a good

Father allow His children to suffer? The parable of the Prodigal Son offers some insights, depicting a father who allows his son to make mistakes and experience consequences, ultimately leading to redemption and restoration. This suggests that God's fatherhood might involve allowing suffering for the sake of growth, free will, and ultimate good. However, this remains one of the most challenging aspects of reconciling God's fatherhood with the realities of human experience.

Understanding God as Father significantly shapes our perception of His character. It emphasizes aspects of God's nature such as love, provision, protection, and even discipline. The father-child relationship implies both care and authority, mirroring the biblical portrayal of God as both merciful and just. This concept helps us grasp God's personal interest in our lives, His desire for relationship, and His commitment to our growth and well-being.

It's worth noting that while other religious traditions may use parental imagery for deities, the Christian concept of God as Father is uniquely personal and relational. In Christianity, God is not just likened to a father but is revealed as The Father, with believers adopted as true children of God. This adoption theology, prominently featured in Paul's letters, underscores the intimacy and permanence of our relationship with God.

The idea of God as Father also informs our understanding of human dignity and worth. If we are all children of God, it implies a fundamental equality and value for all people, regardless of earthly status or circumstances. This has significant implications for ethics, human rights, and how we treat one another.

In conclusion, the theological concept of God as Father is rich with meaning and implications. It offers a deeply personal way of relating to the divine, shapes our understanding of God's character, and influences how we view ourselves and others. While it presents challenges in interpretation and application, particularly in light of contemporary discussions about gender and the problem of suffering, it remains a central and transformative idea in Christian theology.

Psychological and Emotional Impact

The concept of God as Father carries profound psychological and emotional implications for believers. This understanding of the divine can be a source of profound healing, particularly for those who have experienced the pain of absent or abusive earthly fathers. For many, God becomes the ideal Father figure, filling the void left by earthly father wounds. This divine fatherhood offers a consistent, loving, and nurturing presence that can help individuals overcome the trauma and insecurities stemming from difficult paternal relationships.

The idea of God as a loving Father can foster healthy psychological attachment. Attachment theory, a cornerstone of developmental psychology, suggests that a secure relationship with God can provide a stable base for emotional well-being. Just as a child develops a sense of security and self-worth through a healthy relationship with their parents, believers can cultivate a secure attachment to God. This divine attachment can serve as a source of comfort, stability, and resilience in the face of life's challenges.

Understanding oneself as God's child can have a transformative effect on self-perception and identity. Recognizing oneself as a beloved child of God can counteract negative self-talk and low self-esteem. This divine affirmation of worth is not based on personal achievements or societal standards but on the unconditional love of the Creator. For many believers, this realization becomes a powerful antidote to feelings of worthlessness or inadequacy.

However, it's important to acknowledge that for some individuals, the concept of God as Father can present significant challenges. Those who have experienced abuse, neglect, or abandonment from their earthly fathers may initially struggle to relate to God in this way. The journey to seeing God as a loving Father may require healing, reframing, and often professional support. It's a process that demands patience, understanding, and often involves working through deep-seated emotional pain.

The role of the faith community in shaping our understanding of God as Father cannot be overstated. Healthy church communities can provide positive experiences of spiritual fatherhood and family, offering a tangible representation of God's love and care. Through supportive relationships, mentoring, and communal worship, believers can experience aspects of divine fatherhood in human contexts. This communal dimension can be particularly healing for those who lack positive father figures in their personal lives.

Moreover, the concept of God as Father can significantly impact how individuals approach authority, trust, and intimacy in their relationships. As people internalize the attributes of God's perfect fatherhood - such as unconditional love, patient guidance, and consistent presence - they may find themselves better equipped to navigate human relationships. This can lead to improved family dynamics, more trusting friendships, and healthier approaches to leadership and authority.

The psychological benefits of relating to God as Father extend to stress management and emotional regulation. Knowing that one has a divine Father who is always accessible can provide a sense of security and peace in turbulent times. This relationship can become a safe haven, a place of emotional refuge where individuals can bring their fears, doubts, and anxieties.

It's crucial to recognize that the journey of embracing God as Father is often a gradual process, especially for those with complex father relationships. It may involve cycles of progress and setback, requiring patience and self-compassion. Professional counseling, particularly from therapists who understand the integration of faith and psychology, can be invaluable in this journey.

In conclusion, the psychological and emotional impact of understanding God as Father is profound and multifaceted. It offers healing, shapes identity, influences relationships, and provides a framework for emotional well-being. While it can present challenges for some, with proper support and understanding, this concept can be a powerful source of personal transformation and spiritual growth.

Cultural and Historical Perspectives

The concept of God as Father, while revolutionary in Jesus' time, has been shaped and interpreted through various cultural and historical lenses throughout the centuries. To fully appreciate the depth and significance of addressing God as "Our Father," it's crucial to examine these perspectives.

In ancient Near Eastern cultures, fatherhood held a position of paramount importance. The concept of the 'paterfamilias' in ancient Rome, for instance, provides valuable context for understanding the biblical portrayal of God's fatherhood. The paterfamilias held significant authority within the family unit, being responsible for the family's economic well-being, legal matters, and religious practices. This cultural backdrop enriches our understanding of God's fatherhood, highlighting aspects of authority, provision, and spiritual leadership.

However, our perception of fatherhood has not remained static. Over time, significant cultural shifts have influenced how we understand and relate to the concept of God as Father. The industrial revolution marked a turning point in family dynamics, often separating fathers from their children for long periods due to work demands. This shift challenged and reshaped societal understanding of a father's role, inadvertently affecting how people perceived and related to God as Father.

These changes have continued into the modern era, with the concept of fatherhood evolving dramatically. The rise of gender equality movements, changing family structures, and shifting societal norms have all contributed to a reimagining of fatherhood. These cultural changes inevitably influence our theological understanding, prompting deeper reflection on what it means to address God as Father in today's context.

Cross-cultural perspectives add another layer of complexity to this discussion. The way different cultures receive and interpret the concept of God as Father can vary significantly. In some Asian cultures, for example, where filial piety is highly valued, the concept of God as Father carries unique implications. It may emphasize aspects of respect, obedience, and honor in ways that differ from Western interpretations. Understanding these cultural nuances is crucial for global Christianity and interfaith dialogue.

The impact of the sexual revolution and changing family structures in recent decades has further complicated our understanding of God's fatherhood. The rise of single-parent households, same-sex parenting, and other non-traditional family structures has prompted new theological reflections. These societal changes challenge us to consider how the metaphor of God as Father can remain relevant and meaningful in diverse family contexts.

Contemporary theological discussions have also grappled with questions of gender and divinity. The use of masculine language for God, including the term "Father," has been the subject of intense debate. Some theologians argue for more gender-neutral language, suggesting that exclusively male terms for God can reinforce patriarchal structures and alienate those who have experienced abuse from male authority figures. Others maintain that the Father metaphor, as revealed in scripture and taught by Jesus, carries irreplaceable theological significance.

These discussions remind us that while the concept of God as Father is rooted in biblical revelation, our understanding and application of this concept are invariably influenced by our cultural and historical context. As we continue to pray "Our Father," we must remain mindful of these diverse perspectives, allowing them to enrich rather than limit our understanding of God's nature.

Ultimately, the enduring power of addressing God as Father lies in its ability to convey both the intimacy and transcendence of our relationship with the Divine. It invites us into a personal, loving relationship while reminding us of God's authority and care. As we navigate the complexities of modern life and diverse cultural perspectives, the concept of God as Our Father continues to offer a profound framework for understanding our place in relation to the Divine and to one another.

Practical Applications

In this final section, we'll explore practical ways to apply the concept of God as our Father in our daily lives. Understanding God's fatherhood is not merely an intellectual exercise but a transformative truth that should shape our prayers, relationships, and personal growth.

Cultivating intimacy with God through prayer is a fundamental application of this truth. When we approach God as our Father, we're invited into a deeply personal relationship. Try beginning your prayers with "Dear Father" and pause to reflect on the significance of this address. This simple practice can help shift your perspective from viewing prayer as a formal religious duty to an intimate conversation with a loving parent. Consider sharing your deepest fears, hopes, and dreams with God, just as you would with a trustworthy earthly father.

While fostering intimacy, it's crucial to balance this with reverence in worship and daily life. Our understanding of God as Father should never lead to casual or disrespectful attitudes towards Him. Incorporate moments of silent reflection or physical postures of reverence, such as kneeling or bowing, in your prayer time. This can help cultivate a sense of awe and respect for God's majesty and holiness. In your daily life, strive to make decisions and behave in ways that honor God, remembering that you bear His name as His child.

The concept of shared divine fatherhood provides a powerful foundation for fostering unity within the church. Organize or participate in small groups that bring together people from diverse backgrounds, emphasizing your shared identity as God's children. When conflicts arise in your church community, remind yourself and others that you are spiritual siblings, united by the same heavenly Father. This perspective can promote patience, forgiveness, and understanding among believers.

For those struggling with father wounds from earthly relationships, understanding God's perfect fatherhood can be a source of profound healing. If you find yourself grappling with issues related to your earthly father, consider joining a support group or seeking Christian counseling. These resources can help you work through your pain while deepening your understanding of God's unconditional love and perfect fatherhood. Meditate on scriptures that describe God's faithful, loving nature as a Father, allowing these truths to gradually reshape your concept of fatherhood and heal your wounds.

Finally, applying the concept of God's fatherhood to parenting and mentoring relationships can transform how we interact with others, especially those under our care or guidance. Reflect on God's patience, love, and guidance as a model for your own parenting or mentoring style. When faced with challenging situations, ask yourself, "How does God, as a perfect Father, treat me in similar circumstances?" Strive to emulate His unconditional love, gentle correction, and unwavering support in your relationships.

Remember, God's grace empowers us to call Him Father and to grow in our understanding of what that means. As you apply these principles, be patient with yourself and others. Growing in intimacy with God while maintaining reverence is a lifelong journey. Embrace the process, knowing that each step brings you closer to fully experiencing the love of your heavenly Father and reflecting that love to the world around you.

CHAPTER 3: "HALLOWED BE THY NAME": WORSHIPING GOD'S HOLINESS

The Concept of Holiness

T he concept of holiness is foundational to understanding the profound significance of the phrase "hallowed be thy name" in the Lord's Prayer. To truly grasp its meaning, we must first explore the rich tapestry of what it means for something or someone to be holy.

In biblical context, the words "hallowed" and "holy" carry deep significance. The term "holy" derives from the Hebrew word "qadosh," which fundamentally means "set apart" or "distinct." This distinction isn't merely about being different, but about being set apart for a divine purpose. When applied to God, it signifies His utter transcendence and absolute moral purity. To hallow something, then, is to treat it as holy, to set it apart as sacred and worthy of the utmost reverence.

The Jewish tradition has long grappled with the concept of holiness. In ancient Israel, holiness was not an abstract concept but a tangible reality that permeated every aspect of life. The Torah delineates between the holy and the profane, establishing clear boundaries and rituals to maintain this distinction. The

Sabbath, for instance, was set apart as holy time. The Temple in Jerusalem, particularly the Holy of Holies, was understood as holy space. Even certain objects and people – like the Ark of the Covenant or the priests – were designated as holy.

As we transition to the New Testament perspective, we see both continuity and transformation in the understanding of holiness. Jesus, while upholding the sanctity of God's holiness, also radically redefined it. He taught that true holiness wasn't just about external rituals but about the condition of one's heart. The Apostle Peter echoes this sentiment when he exhorts believers to "be holy in all your conduct" (1 Peter 1:15), emphasizing that holiness should permeate every aspect of a Christian's life.

Theologically, God's holiness is not just one attribute among many, but the very essence of His character. It encompasses His absolute moral perfection, His transcendent majesty, and His utter "otherness" from creation. As theologian R.C. Sproul famously put it, God is not just "the Holy One," He is "the Holy, Holy, Holy One," emphasizing the superlative nature of His holiness.

In contemporary culture, however, the concept of holiness is often misunderstood or diluted. Some equate holiness with a dour, joyless piety, while others reduce it to mere moral behavior. Still others dismiss it entirely as an outdated religious concept. Yet, a proper understanding of holiness reveals it to be both awe-inspiring and deeply attractive – it's about participating in the very life and character of God.

The concept of holiness, therefore, is not a relic of religious history but a vital, transformative reality. When we pray "hallowed be thy name," we're not just uttering pious words, but aligning ourselves with the awesome reality of God's holiness. We're acknowledging His utter transcendence while also inviting His holy presence to permeate every aspect of our lives. This understanding sets the stage for a deeper exploration of what it means to truly hallow God's name in our prayers and in our lives.

God's Name in Biblical Tradition

The concept of a name holds profound significance in ancient Near Eastern culture, far beyond mere identification. Names were believed to embody the essence, character, and destiny of an individual or deity. In this context, the names of God revealed in the Old Testament take on extraordinary importance, offering glimpses into the divine nature and relationship with humanity.

Throughout the Hebrew Scriptures, God is known by various names, each revealing a different aspect of His character. El Shaddai, often translated as "God Almighty," speaks to His omnipotence and sufficiency. Adonai, meaning "Lord" or "Master," emphasizes His sovereignty. El Elyon, "God Most High," underscores His supremacy over all creation. These names, among others, paint a multifaceted portrait of the divine, inviting worshippers to engage with different facets of God's nature.

Perhaps the most significant and mysterious of God's names in the Old Testament is the Tetragrammaton, YHWH. This four-letter name, believed to be derived from the Hebrew verb "to be," was considered so holy that it was rarely spoken aloud. Instead, it was often substituted with "Adonai" in reading and speech. The revelation of this name to Moses at the burning bush (Exodus 3:14) marks a pivotal moment in biblical history, signifying God's self-disclosure and covenant relationship with His people.

The significance of YHWH lies not just in its sacred status but in its meaning. Often rendered as "I AM WHO I AM" or "I WILL BE WHAT I WILL BE," it speaks to God's self-existence, immutability, and faithfulness. This name became central to Jewish identity and worship, embodying the unique monotheistic faith of Israel amidst a polytheistic ancient world.

When we turn to the New Testament, we encounter a striking shift in how God is addressed. Jesus consistently refers to God as "Father," and teaches His disciples to do the same. This intimate form of address was revolutionary, reflecting the new covenant relationship made possible through Christ. The Aramaic term "Abba," used by Jesus in His prayers, conveys a sense of closeness and trust that was unprecedented in Jewish tradition.

Jesus' use of "Father" does not replace or diminish the significance of God's other names but rather adds a new dimension to our understanding of the divine. It invites believers into a relationship characterized by both reverence and intimacy, awe and affection.

The implications of knowing and using God's name are profound. In biblical thought, to know someone's name implied a level of relationship and even authority. By revealing His names to humanity, God invites us into a deep, personal relationship. At the same time, the privilege of knowing God's name comes with responsibility. The Third Commandment warns against misusing God's name, underscoring the reverence with which it should be treated.

In our modern context, where names are often treated casually, recovering a sense of the sacredness of God's name can transform our approach to prayer and worship. It calls us to approach God with a balance of confidence and humility, intimacy and reverence. Whether we address God as Father, Lord, or by another biblical name, we do so with the awareness that we are engaging with the infinite, eternal Creator who has chosen to make Himself known to us.

Understanding the rich tradition of God's names in Scripture deepens our appreciation of the phrase "hallowed be thy name" in the Lord's Prayer. It is not merely a polite acknowledgment but a profound recognition of God's holiness and an commitment to honor that holiness in our lives. As we pray these words, we align ourselves with a long tradition of believers who have sought to revere and glorify the name of God in their worship and daily living.

Hallowing God's Name in Prayer

The phrase "hallowed be thy name" stands at the heart of the Lord's Prayer, inviting us to consider deeply what it means to sanctify God's name through our words and actions. To fully grasp the significance of this phrase, we must first examine its original Greek formulation: "ἁγιασθήτω τὸ ὄνομά σου" (hagiasthētō to onoma sou).

This Greek phrase employs a passive imperative verb, which can be literally translated as "let your name be made holy." The use of the passive voice is significant, as it implies that the action of hallowing is not something we do directly, but rather something we allow to happen or participate in. This grammatical construction underscores the idea that God's name is inherently holy, and our role is to recognize, respect, and reflect that holiness in our lives and prayers.

The concept of hallowing God's name is not unique to the Lord's Prayer. Similar phrases can be found in Jewish prayers, particularly in the Kaddish, which begins with "Magnified and sanctified be His great name." This parallel highlights the deep roots of this idea in the Judeo-Christian tradition and emphasizes its central importance in our approach to God.

The passive divine construction used in "hallowed be thy name" carries profound theological implications. It suggests that while we are called to participate in the hallowing of God's name, the ultimate source of holiness is God Himself. Our role is to align ourselves with God's holiness, allowing it to transform us and, through us, the world around us.

This phrase in the Lord's Prayer also resonates strongly with the

Third Commandment, which instructs us not to take the Lord's name in vain. By praying for God's name to be hallowed, we are committing ourselves to honor and revere God's name in all aspects of our lives. It's a recognition that how we speak of and relate to God has significant spiritual and ethical implications.

In practical terms, hallowing God's name in prayer invites us to approach our communication with God with a sense of reverence and awe. It calls us to be mindful of the words we use, the attitudes we bring, and the intentions behind our prayers. This doesn't mean that our prayers should be formal or stilted; rather, it suggests that even in our most intimate conversations with God, we should maintain an awareness of His transcendent holiness.

For personal prayer, this might mean taking time to center ourselves and acknowledge God's holiness before launching into our requests or concerns. It could involve incorporating praise and adoration into our prayer routine, not just as a formality, but as a genuine expression of our recognition of God's holy nature.

In communal prayer settings, hallowing God's name might be reflected in the careful preparation of liturgy, the reverent use of sacred spaces, or the thoughtful selection of music and readings that honor God's holiness. It might also involve fostering an atmosphere of respect and attentiveness during worship services.

Ultimately, praying "hallowed be thy name" is not just about the words we say, but about cultivating a lifestyle that consistently honors God's holiness. It's a commitment to live in such a way that our actions, choices, and relationships reflect the sacred nature of the God we serve. By doing so, we participate in making God's name holy in the world, fulfilling the very prayer we utter.

As we continue to explore the Lord's Prayer, this understanding of hallowing God's name serves as a foundation for how we approach the subsequent petitions. It sets the tone for our entire relationship with God, reminding us that even as we bring our needs and desires before Him, we do so in the context of His supreme holiness and majesty.

Worship and Reverence

The act of hallowing God's name is intrinsically linked to worship and reverence. When we declare "hallowed be thy name" in the Lord's Prayer, we are not merely uttering words, but engaging in an act of worship that acknowledges God's supreme holiness and our reverent response to it.

The connection between hallowing God's name and worship is profound and multifaceted. At its core, worship is our human response to the divine revelation of God's character and actions. When we truly understand the holiness of God's name, our natural response is one of awe, wonder, and adoration. This response manifests itself in various forms of worship, from silent contemplation to exuberant praise.

Different Christian traditions have developed unique forms of reverence in their worship practices. In Orthodox traditions, for instance, the use of icons, incense, and elaborate liturgies creates an atmosphere of mystery and transcendence that emphasizes God's holiness. In contrast, many Protestant traditions focus on the Word, emphasizing reverent study and application of Scripture as a way of honoring God's name. Catholic traditions often blend these approaches, incorporating both sacramental reverence and scriptural focus. Despite these differences, the underlying goal remains the same: to approach God with a sense of His holiness and to respond appropriately.

One of the challenges in modern Christian spirituality is balancing intimacy with God and maintaining a sense of reverence. The biblical narrative presents God as both a loving Father and a holy, transcendent Being. Jesus taught His disciples to address God as "Our Father," inviting a level of intimacy previously unheard of in Jewish tradition. However, this intimacy is immediately followed by "hallowed be thy name," reminding us that our loving Father is also the Holy One.

Striking this balance requires wisdom and discernment. While we are encouraged to approach God's throne of grace with confidence (Hebrews 4:16), we must never lose sight of the fact that we are created beings addressing the Creator of the universe. This balance can be achieved through practices that foster both intimacy and reverence, such as contemplative prayer, studying God's attributes, and engaging in corporate worship that includes elements of both joy and solemnity.

The role of awe and wonder in spiritual life cannot be overstated. These emotions are not merely fleeting feelings but are central to a vibrant faith. When we encounter God's holiness, it should evoke in us a sense of awe - a mixture of fear and fascination, of being overwhelmed yet drawn in. This experience of awe has the power to transform our perspective, helping us see our lives and the world around us in light of God's grandeur and holiness.

Cultivating a sense of the sacred in a secular world presents both challenges and opportunities. In a culture that often trivializes the divine and dismisses the concept of holiness, intentionally creating space for reverence becomes a countercultural act. This might involve setting aside specific times and places for worship, adopting practices that remind us of God's presence throughout the day, or deliberately using language that reflects the honor due to God's name.

Moreover, cultivating reverence isn't limited to explicitly religious activities. We can bring a sense of the sacred into our everyday lives by approaching our work, relationships, and even mundane tasks with an awareness of God's holiness. This might mean treating others with respect as bearers of God's image, pursuing excellence in our work as an offering to God, or pausing to appreciate the beauty of creation as a reflection of its

Creator.

In conclusion, worship and reverence are essential components of hallowing God's name. They remind us of our place in relation to the Divine, inspire us to live lives worthy of our calling, and draw us into a deeper, more transformative relationship with the Holy One. As we learn to balance intimacy and reverence, cultivate awe and wonder, and infuse our daily lives with a sense of the sacred, we participate in the ongoing act of hallowing God's name, fulfilling the prayer that Jesus taught us to pray.

Living Out God's Holiness

The concept of hallowing God's name extends far beyond mere words or ritualistic practices. It encompasses a profound call to embody God's holiness in our daily lives. This section explores the practical implications of living out God's holiness and the transformative power it holds for individuals and communities.

At the heart of this pursuit lies the biblical injunction to "be holy as God is holy." This commandment, found in both the Old and New Testaments, serves as a foundational principle for Christian ethics and behavior. It challenges believers to reflect God's character in their thoughts, actions, and interactions with others. This call to holiness is not about achieving moral perfection, but rather about aligning one's life with the divine nature and purposes.

The ethical implications of hallowing God's name are far-reaching. It demands integrity in all areas of life, from personal relationships to business dealings. When we truly reverence God's name, we are compelled to act justly, love mercy, and walk humbly with our Creator. This ethical framework shapes our decisions, influencing how we treat others, steward resources, and engage with societal issues.

Representing God's holiness in daily life requires intentionality and mindfulness. It involves cultivating virtues such as compassion, patience, and selflessness. In a world often characterized by self-interest and instant gratification, living out God's holiness stands as a powerful counter-cultural witness. It may manifest in acts of kindness, speaking truth in love, or choosing forgiveness over resentment.

However, the challenge of holiness in a morally complex world cannot be overstated. We often face situations where the "right" course of action is not immediately clear. Ethical dilemmas in professional settings, conflicting loyalties in relationships, or navigating political disagreements all present opportunities to live out God's holiness. In these moments, we are called to seek wisdom, exercise discernment, and remain faithful to our commitment to honor God's name.

To illustrate the transformative power of living out God's holiness, consider the story of William Wilberforce. This 18th-century British politician dedicated his life to abolishing the slave trade, motivated by his deep Christian faith and understanding of God's holiness. Despite facing immense opposition and personal cost, Wilberforce persevered in his efforts for decades. His unwavering commitment to justice and human dignity, rooted in his reverence for God's holy name, ultimately led to the abolition of slavery in the British Empire.

Another inspiring example is that of Mother Teresa, whose work among the poorest of the poor in Calcutta exemplified a life wholly devoted to hallowing God's name. Her selfless service, compassion, and love for those society often overlooked reflected the holiness of God in tangible ways. Mother Teresa's life demonstrates how living out God's holiness can have a profound impact on individuals and communities.

These stories remind us that hallowing God's name through our lives is not reserved for spiritual giants or historical figures. Everyday individuals can embody God's holiness in meaningful ways. A teacher who goes the extra mile to support struggling students, a business owner who prioritizes ethical practices over profit, or a neighbor who consistently offers help and kindness to those around them – all these are examples of living out God's holiness in daily life.

Ultimately, the call to live out God's holiness is an invitation to a transformative journey. It challenges us to continually grow in our understanding of God's character and to align our lives with His purposes. As we strive to hallow God's name through our actions and attitudes, we not only honor our Creator but also become agents of positive change in the world around us. This pursuit of holiness, grounded in reverence for God's name, has the power to reshape individuals, communities, and even societies, reflecting the beauty and goodness of our holy God.

Hallowing God's Name in Different Contexts

The call to hallow God's name extends far beyond the confines of a church building or the quiet moments of personal prayer. It permeates every aspect of our lives, challenging us to live out this sacred mandate in diverse settings and situations. This section explores how we can honor God's holiness in various contexts of our daily lives.

In personal spirituality, hallowing God's name begins with cultivating a deep sense of reverence and awe in our individual relationship with the Divine. This might involve setting aside dedicated time for contemplation, studying scripture with a focus on God's character, or engaging in spiritual practices that heighten our awareness of God's presence. For instance, the ancient practice of lectio divina, or sacred reading, can help us approach biblical texts with a sense of holy expectation, allowing God's word to transform our hearts and minds.

Family life presents both unique challenges and opportunities for hallowing God's name. In the hustle and bustle of daily routines, it's easy to lose sight of the sacred. However, families can intentionally create spaces and rituals that honor God's holiness. This might include regular family devotions, blessing children in God's name, or fostering an atmosphere of gratitude and wonder at God's creation. For example, a family might choose to say grace before meals, not as a rote exercise, but as a meaningful acknowledgment of God's provision and an opportunity to teach children about reverence.

Professional settings often seem far removed from matters of faith, yet they provide crucial opportunities for hallowing God's name. This doesn't necessarily mean overt evangelism, but rather living out one's faith through integrity, excellence, and compassion. A business leader might hallow God's name by ensuring ethical practices throughout their organization. A teacher could do so by treating each student with dignity and nurturing their God-given potential. A healthcare worker might honor God's holiness through compassionate care that recognizes the divine image in each patient.

In public discourse, hallowing God's name takes on particular importance and complexity. In an era of polarized debates and social media echo chambers, Christians are called to engage in ways that reflect God's character. This means speaking truth with love, listening with humility, and seeking the common good rather than partisan advantage. It might involve advocating for justice and mercy in public policy, or simply modeling respectful dialogue in online interactions.

Interfaith dialogue presents a unique context for hallowing God's name. While remaining true to one's own faith convictions, engaging with those of different beliefs can be an opportunity to demonstrate the love and holiness of God. This might involve finding common ground on shared values, showing genuine interest in understanding others' perspectives, and embodying the peace and reconciliation central to the Christian message. For instance, participating in interfaith community service projects can be a powerful way to honor God's name alongside those of different faiths.

In each of these contexts, hallowing God's name is not about grand gestures or religious showmanship. Rather, it's about a consistent, authentic living out of faith that reflects the character of a holy God. It's about allowing the reality of God's holiness to permeate our actions, attitudes, and interactions in every sphere of life.

As we navigate these various contexts, we're reminded that hallowing God's name is both a privilege and a responsibility. It's an ongoing process of aligning our lives with the holiness of God, allowing His character to shine through our words and deeds. Whether in the privacy of our homes, the busyness of our workplaces, or the complexity of public life, we are called to be living testimonies to the holiness of our God.

Contemporary Challenges and Opportunities

In our modern world, the concept of hallowing God's name faces both unique challenges and exciting opportunities. As we navigate the complexities of the 21st century, we must consider how this fundamental aspect of the Lord's Prayer intersects with contemporary issues and mindsets.

The process of secularization has significantly impacted how society at large views the concept of holiness. In many parts of the world, particularly in Western countries, there has been a gradual erosion of religious influence in public life. This shift has led to a diminished understanding and appreciation of the sacred among the general population. However, this challenge also presents an opportunity for believers to reintroduce the concept of holiness in fresh, relevant ways. By demonstrating the value of recognizing something greater than ourselves, we can invite others to explore the transformative power of hallowing God's name.

The digital age has brought about unprecedented connectivity and access to information, but it has also created new challenges for maintaining a sense of the sacred. Social media platforms and constant digital stimulation can make it difficult to cultivate the quiet, reverent spaces necessary for truly hallowing God's name. Yet, these same technologies offer innovative ways to share and explore spiritual practices. Online prayer groups, devotional apps, and virtual faith communities can help individuals incorporate the hallowing of God's name into their daily digital lives.

Environmental stewardship has emerged as a critical issue in recent decades, and it provides a powerful context for hallowing God's name. By recognizing the earth as God's creation, we can approach environmental conservation as an act of reverence. Caring for the planet becomes not just a matter of ecological necessity, but a way of honoring the Creator. This perspective can inspire believers to lead the charge in addressing climate change and promoting sustainable practices as an expression of their faith.

The pursuit of social justice is another arena where hallowing God's name finds contemporary expression. As we recognize God's holiness, we are compelled to reflect that holiness in our treatment of others. This understanding can motivate believers to actively work against inequality, discrimination, and oppression. By striving to create a more just and equitable society, we honor God's name and make His holiness visible in the world.

In our increasingly casual culture, there is a growing need to rediscover the value of reverence. The informality that characterizes many aspects of modern life can sometimes seep into our spiritual practices, potentially diminishing our sense of God's holiness. However, this cultural shift also offers an opportunity to explore new ways of expressing reverence that feel authentic and meaningful to contemporary believers. We can seek to strike a balance between approachability and awe in our relationship with God, finding fresh language and practices that convey deep respect without feeling artificial or outdated.

As we face these contemporary challenges and opportunities,

we are called to creatively and authentically hallow God's name in ways that resonate with our current context. By doing so, we not only enrich our own spiritual lives but also offer a compelling witness to the relevance and power of recognizing God's holiness in today's world. Whether through digital platforms, environmental activism, pursuit of social justice, or cultivating reverence in our daily lives, we have countless avenues to make the hallowing of God's name a vibrant, transformative practice in the 21st century.

CHAPTER 4: "THY KINGDOM COME": ALIGNING WITH GOD'S WILL AND PURPOSES

Understanding "The Kingdom of God"

T he concept of "The Kingdom of God" lies at the heart of Jesus' teachings and forms a cornerstone of Christian theology. To fully grasp the significance of praying "Thy Kingdom Come," we must first explore what this Kingdom entails and how it has been understood throughout biblical history.

In its essence, the Kingdom of God refers to God's sovereign rule and reign over all creation. This concept has deep roots in Jewish thought, dating back to the Old Testament. The ancient Israelites understood God as their true King, even when human monarchs ruled over them. They anticipated a time when God's rule would be fully realized on earth, bringing about perfect justice, peace, and harmony.

As Judaism evolved, particularly during the intertestamental period, the expectation of a Messianic Kingdom gained prominence. Many Jews longed for a divinely appointed leader who would restore Israel's political autonomy and usher in an era of spiritual renewal. This hope was especially fervent during the time of Roman occupation when Jesus began his ministry.

Jesus' teachings on the Kingdom of God both built upon and radically reinterpreted these existing expectations. He spoke of the Kingdom as something both present and future, already here but not yet fully realized. In parables and direct teachings, Jesus described the Kingdom as a reality that was breaking into the world through his own presence and ministry.

One of the most striking aspects of Jesus' Kingdom message was its present reality. He declared, "The Kingdom of God is at hand" (Mark 1:15), suggesting that God's reign was not merely a future hope but a current reality that people could enter into and experience. This present aspect of the Kingdom was manifest in Jesus' miraculous healings, his authority over evil spirits, and the transformation of lives through his teaching and forgiveness.

However, Jesus also spoke of the Kingdom as something yet to come in its fullness. He taught his disciples to pray for the Kingdom's coming, implying its future consummation. This tension between the "already" and "not yet" aspects of the Kingdom has been a central feature of Christian theology and spirituality throughout the centuries.

The Kingdom of God was not just one among many themes in Jesus' ministry; it was the central motif that unified his entire message and mission. His proclamation that "the Kingdom of God is at hand" served as the foundation for his call to repentance and faith. His parables frequently began with the phrase, "The Kingdom of God is like..." as he sought to help his listeners grasp this revolutionary concept.

Understanding the Kingdom of God as Jesus taught it is crucial for interpreting the Lord's Prayer. When we pray "Thy Kingdom

Come," we are not merely asking for a future event but aligning ourselves with God's present activity in the world. We are acknowledging God's sovereignty and expressing our desire to see his rule extend more fully into every aspect of human existence.

This Kingdom understanding challenges us to view the world differently. It calls us to recognize God's active presence and work in our midst, even amid circumstances that seem to contradict his reign. It invites us to participate in God's redemptive mission, becoming agents of his Kingdom values in our families, communities, and societies.

As we delve deeper into the implications of praying for God's Kingdom to come, we must keep in mind this rich biblical and theological background. The Kingdom of God is not just a future hope but a present reality, not merely a spiritual concept but a force for transformation in every sphere of life. It is this multifaceted understanding of the Kingdom that gives the phrase "Thy Kingdom Come" its profound and revolutionary significance in the Lord's Prayer.

The Revolutionary Nature of "Thy Kingdom Come"

The phrase "Thy Kingdom Come" carries with it a deeply revolutionary connotation, particularly when viewed through the lens of its historical context. In the world of Roman-occupied Judea, where Jesus taught this prayer, these words held profound political implications. The very concept of a kingdom other than Caesar's was treasonous, yet Jesus boldly proclaimed a higher allegiance.

This revolutionary nature of the Kingdom prayer directly challenged earthly power structures. It suggested that there was an authority beyond that of Rome, beyond any human government or ruler. In praying for God's Kingdom to come, believers were essentially declaring that the current systems and structures were not ultimate, and that a greater, more perfect order was on its way.

The Kingdom Jesus spoke of represented both a spiritual and social transformation. Unlike earthly revolutions that often merely replace one flawed system with another, the coming of God's Kingdom promised a fundamental reshaping of reality itself. This Kingdom wasn't just about changing who was in charge, but about altering the very nature of power, justice, and human relationships.

When contrasted with human kingdoms and empires, the differences become stark. Earthly kingdoms are often built on force, coercion, and the consolidation of power and wealth. God's Kingdom, as described by Jesus, operates on radically different principles – love, service, humility, and self-sacrifice. Where human empires seek to dominate, God's Kingdom seeks to liberate and elevate.

The values of the Kingdom are fundamentally countercultural. In a world that often celebrates strength, wealth, and status, the Kingdom elevates the poor in spirit, the meek, and those who hunger and thirst for righteousness. It calls for loving one's enemies, forgiving without limit, and finding greatness through servanthood. These teachings turn conventional wisdom on its head and challenge deeply ingrained societal norms.

Praying "Thy Kingdom Come" is thus not a passive plea, but a radical commitment to a different way of living and viewing the world. It's a recognition that the current state of affairs – both personally and globally – is not aligned with God's perfect will, and an active petition for transformative change. It's a prayer that, if taken seriously, demands nothing less than a complete reorientation of one's life and priorities.

This revolutionary aspect of the Kingdom prayer serves as a constant reminder that as followers of Christ, we are called to be agents of change in this world. We are not to simply accept things as they are, but to actively work towards aligning our personal lives, our communities, and our world with the values and principles of God's Kingdom. It challenges us to critically examine our own allegiances, to question unjust systems, and to courageously stand for truth and righteousness, even when it goes against the prevailing cultural tide.

In essence, praying "Thy Kingdom Come" is a revolutionary act of hope and defiance. It's an affirmation that despite the brokenness we see around us, we believe in and actively anticipate a better world – one that fully embodies God's love, justice, and peace. It's a commitment to being part of that divine revolution, allowing God's Kingdom to take root in our hearts and spread outward, transforming everything it touches.

"Thy Will Be Done": Surrendering to Divine Purpose

The phrase "Thy will be done" in the Lord's Prayer is inextricably linked to the concept of God's Kingdom. This connection emphasizes that the coming of God's Kingdom is not merely about a change in external circumstances, but a profound alignment with God's purposes and desires.

This idea finds a poignant parallel in Jesus' own prayer in the Garden of Gethsemane. Facing the prospect of crucifixion, Jesus prayed, "Father, if you are willing, take this cup from me; yet not my will, but yours be done" (Luke 22:42). This moment of surrender exemplifies the essence of "Thy will be done" – a willingness to set aside personal desires in favor of God's greater plan.

The challenge inherent in this part of the prayer is significant. It calls us to align our personal desires, ambitions, and plans with God's will. This alignment often requires a radical reorientation of our priorities and a willingness to surrender control. It invites us to trust that God's plans, while sometimes mysterious or challenging, are ultimately for our good and the good of all creation.

The phrase "on earth as it is in heaven" further elaborates on this concept. It suggests that our prayer is for the perfect will of God, as it exists in heaven, to be manifest in our earthly reality. This bridging of the divine-human gap is a central aspiration of the Christian faith. It acknowledges that while we live in a world often marked by discord, suffering, and injustice, we are called to actively participate in bringing about a reality that more closely reflects God's perfect will.

This participation is not passive. Praying "Thy will be done" is not an invitation to inaction or fatalism. Rather, it's a commitment to active engagement in discerning and carrying out God's purposes. It calls us to be attentive to God's guidance, to study Scripture, to engage in prayer and meditation, and to act in ways that align with what we understand of God's character and desires.

In practical terms, this might mean making choices that prioritize compassion over self-interest, justice over personal gain, or long-term sustainability over short-term profit. It could involve forgiving someone who has wronged us, standing up for the marginalized, or making personal sacrifices for the greater good. Each of these actions, in its own way, helps to manifest God's will "on earth as it is in heaven."

Moreover, "Thy will be done" is a recognition of our limited perspective. It's an admission that our understanding is finite, while God's wisdom is infinite. This humility opens us up to new possibilities and perspectives, allowing us to see beyond our immediate circumstances to the broader tapestry of God's plan.

Ultimately, praying for God's will to be done is an act of trust and surrender. It's an acknowledgment that God's ways are higher than our ways, and God's thoughts higher than our thoughts (Isaiah 55:9). This surrender, far from being a weakness, is a source of strength and peace. It frees us from the burden of trying to control every aspect of our lives and allows us to rest in the assurance of God's overarching care and purpose.

As we pray "Thy will be done," we align ourselves with the very heartbeat of creation, participating in the grand narrative of God's redemptive work in the world. We become co-creators with God, instruments of divine purpose, helping to usher in the fullness of God's Kingdom "on earth as it is in heaven."

The Kingdom's Impact on Personal Transformation

The prayer "Thy Kingdom Come" isn't just about global or cosmic change; it's also a powerful catalyst for personal transformation. As we align ourselves with God's kingdom, we experience a profound reshaping of our individual priorities and values. This transformation begins in the heart and mind, gradually extending to every aspect of our lives.

When we prioritize God's kingdom, we naturally start to reevaluate what truly matters. Material possessions, social status, and worldly success begin to lose their grip on our hearts. Instead, we find ourselves increasingly drawn to pursuits that align with kingdom values – compassion, justice, humility, and love. This shift in priorities isn't always easy, but it brings a deep sense of purpose and fulfillment that far outweighs any temporary discomfort.

Cultivating a Kingdom-minded character becomes a central focus of our personal growth. We begin to see ourselves not just as individuals seeking our own good, but as citizens of God's kingdom, called to embody its values in our daily lives. This perspective encourages us to develop virtues such as patience, kindness, forgiveness, and selflessness. We start to view challenges and relationships through the lens of kingdom principles, asking ourselves, "How would a citizen of God's kingdom respond in this situation?"

Living in anticipation of the Kingdom's fullness adds a unique dimension to our personal journey. While we recognize that the complete realization of God's kingdom is yet to come, we live with a sense of hopeful expectation. This anticipation isn't passive; rather, it energizes us to actively participate in bringing glimpses of the kingdom into our present reality. We become more attuned to opportunities to demonstrate God's love, justice, and mercy in our spheres of influence.

However, this forward-looking perspective also presents a challenge: balancing our present responsibilities with our future hope. We must navigate the tension of being fully engaged in our current world while maintaining an eternal perspective. This balance requires wisdom and discernment. We're called to be responsible citizens, employees, family members, and community members, all while keeping our ultimate citizenship in God's kingdom at the forefront of our minds.

To cultivate this kingdom-oriented life, many find it helpful to adopt specific spiritual practices. Regular prayer and meditation on Scripture help us internalize kingdom values and maintain our focus on God's purposes. Acts of service and generosity allow us to tangibly express kingdom principles. Participating in a community of faith provides support, accountability, and opportunities for collective kingdom living.

Fasting can be another powerful tool for personal transformation, helping us break free from worldly attachments and intensify our spiritual focus. Some find it beneficial to periodically "fast" from social media, entertainment, or other distractions to create more space for kingdom-centered reflection and action.

Ultimately, the impact of praying "Thy Kingdom Come" on personal transformation is profound and far-reaching. It challenges us to continual growth, inviting us to align every aspect of our lives – our thoughts, actions, relationships, and aspirations – with the values and purposes of God's kingdom. As we embrace this transformation, we not only experience personal renewal but also become more effective agents of kingdom change in the world around us. Our lives become living testimonies to the reality and power of God's kingdom, inviting others to experience its transformative impact for themselves.

Social and Communal Implications of the Kingdom

The prayer "Thy Kingdom Come" extends far beyond individual spiritual transformation, carrying profound implications for our social structures and communal life. As we delve into the social and communal aspects of God's Kingdom, we uncover a vision for society that challenges our current norms and invites us to participate in a radical reimagining of human relationships and societal priorities.

At the heart of the Kingdom's social vision is a call for justice. This is not merely about fair legal systems, but a comprehensive understanding of justice that permeates every aspect of society. The prophets of the Old Testament frequently tied the coming of God's Kingdom to the establishment of justice, particularly for the marginalized and oppressed. Jesus continued this theme, often associating the Kingdom with good news for the poor and liberation for the captives. When we pray for God's Kingdom to come, we are implicitly praying for a world where injustice is abolished, where the weak are protected, and where every person is treated with the dignity befitting a bearer of God's image.

The economic implications of Kingdom values are equally revolutionary. In a world often driven by greed and self-interest, the Kingdom presents an alternative economic model based on generosity, stewardship, and the belief that all resources ultimately belong to God. Jesus' teachings frequently touched on economic matters, challenging the accumulation of wealth for its own sake and promoting a spirit of radical generosity. The early Christian community, as described in the book of Acts, took these teachings to heart, sharing possessions and ensuring that no one among them was in need. While the specific application may vary in different contexts, the underlying principle remains: in God's Kingdom, economic systems serve the common good rather than concentrating wealth in the hands of a few.

Transforming relationships and communities is another crucial aspect of the Kingdom's social impact. Jesus' teachings on love, forgiveness, and reconciliation provide a blueprint for human interactions that stand in stark contrast to the often divisive and self-centered nature of human relationships. In the Kingdom, enemies are loved, offenses are forgiven, and reconciliation is actively pursued. Communities shaped by these values become beacons of hope, demonstrating the possibility of genuine unity amidst diversity and offering a foretaste of the perfect communion that will characterize the fully realized Kingdom.

Environmental stewardship emerges as a significant Kingdom mandate when we consider the scope of God's reign. The biblical narrative begins in a garden and ends with the renewal of all creation. As such, caring for the environment is not peripheral but central to Kingdom living. When we pray for God's will to be done "on earth as it is in heaven," we are praying for the restoration and flourishing of the entire created order. This challenges us to re-evaluate our relationship with nature, moving from exploitation to responsible stewardship and care for the planet that God has entrusted to us.

Finally, the Church itself is called to be a foretaste of the coming Kingdom. While imperfect, the Christian community should strive to embody Kingdom values in its internal life and its engagement with the wider world. This involves creating communities characterized by love, justice, and reconciliation, where the values of the Kingdom are lived out in practical ways. It also involves being a prophetic voice in society, advocating for Kingdom principles in public life and demonstrating an alternative way of living that challenges the status quo.

The social and communal implications of praying "Thy Kingdom Come" are far-reaching and deeply challenging. They call us to a radical reorientation of our priorities, a transformation of our relationships, and a commitment to being agents of God's justice and love in the world. As we embrace these Kingdom values, we participate in God's ongoing work of renewal, becoming living testimonies to the reality of the Kingdom that is both already here and still to come in its fullness.

Challenges and Tensions in Seeking the Kingdom

Seeking the Kingdom of God is not without its challenges and tensions. As believers strive to align their lives with God's will and purposes, they often encounter difficulties that test their faith and resolve.

One of the primary challenges is balancing an otherworldly focus with earthly engagement. The call to seek first the Kingdom of God can sometimes lead to an excessive detachment from worldly affairs, resulting in a neglect of important earthly responsibilities. Conversely, becoming too engrossed in earthly matters can distract from the pursuit of God's Kingdom. Striking the right balance requires wisdom and discernment, as followers of Christ are called to be "in the world but not of the world."

Another significant tension arises from navigating diverse interpretations of the Kingdom. Throughout history, Christians have held varying views on the nature and manifestation of God's Kingdom. Some emphasize its present reality, while others focus on its future fulfillment. Some interpret it primarily in spiritual terms, while others see it as having concrete social and political implications. These differing perspectives can lead to disagreements and divisions within the Christian community. It's crucial for believers to approach these differences with humility and grace, recognizing that our understanding of God's Kingdom may be limited and that we can learn from one another.

Patience and perseverance in awaiting the Kingdom's fullness present another challenge. Jesus taught that the Kingdom is both "already" and "not yet" - present in part but not yet fully realized. This tension can be difficult to navigate, especially when faced with the harsh realities of a world that often seems far from God's ideal. Believers must cultivate patience, trusting in God's timing and purposes while actively working to manifest Kingdom values in the present.

Dealing with disappointment when the Kingdom seems distant is a common struggle for many Christians. In times of personal hardship, global crises, or widespread injustice, it can be challenging to hold onto the hope of God's coming Kingdom. These moments of doubt and disappointment require a deep-rooted faith and a community of believers to provide support and encouragement.

Responding to skepticism about the Kingdom's reality is another challenge that believers face. In an increasingly secular world, the concept of God's Kingdom can seem outdated or irrelevant to many. Christians must be prepared to articulate the relevance and transformative power of the Kingdom message in ways that resonate with contemporary society. This requires not only a deep understanding of Kingdom theology but also an ability to demonstrate its practical implications through lived experience.

Moreover, the tension between the "already" and "not yet" aspects of the Kingdom can lead to confusion and frustration. Believers may struggle with questions about why God allows suffering and evil to persist if His Kingdom is already present.

Grappling with these theological and existential questions is part of the journey of faith, requiring ongoing study, prayer, and community dialogue.

Additionally, the call to live by Kingdom values often puts believers at odds with prevailing cultural norms and societal expectations. This can lead to personal and professional conflicts, as Kingdom priorities may clash with worldly ambitions or social pressures. Navigating these conflicts while maintaining integrity and witness to the Kingdom requires courage, wisdom, and often sacrifice.

Finally, there's the challenge of maintaining hope and enthusiasm for the Kingdom in the face of apparent setbacks or slow progress. The gradual nature of Kingdom growth, as illustrated in Jesus' parables, can be discouraging for those expecting rapid or dramatic change. Cultivating a long-term perspective and celebrating small victories becomes crucial in sustaining Kingdom-focused living.

Despite these challenges and tensions, the pursuit of God's Kingdom remains central to the Christian faith. These difficulties, when approached with faith and perseverance, can deepen one's understanding of God's ways and strengthen commitment to His purposes. As believers navigate these tensions, they are refined and shaped, becoming more effective ambassadors of the Kingdom they seek.

Contemporary Relevance and Application

In our modern world, the prayer "Thy Kingdom Come" takes on renewed significance, offering a powerful antidote to the pervasive materialism that often dominates our societies. As we grapple with the allure of consumerism and the relentless pursuit of wealth, this Kingdom-focused petition serves as a poignant reminder of higher values and eternal purposes. It challenges us to recalibrate our priorities, shifting our focus from accumulating earthly possessions to cultivating spiritual riches that align with God's will.

The principles of God's Kingdom provide a compelling framework for addressing contemporary social issues. In a world marked by inequality, injustice, and conflict, the Kingdom's emphasis on love, justice, and reconciliation offers a transformative approach to societal challenges. By applying Kingdom values to areas such as poverty alleviation, racial reconciliation, and environmental stewardship, we can work towards creating a more just and equitable world that reflects God's intentions for humanity.

Living out the prayer "Thy Kingdom Come" in a pluralistic society presents both challenges and opportunities. While respecting the diverse beliefs of others, we are called to embody Kingdom values in our interactions, decisions, and lifestyle choices. This might involve advocating for policies that promote human dignity, engaging in interfaith dialogue with grace and conviction, or simply demonstrating Christ-like love and compassion in our daily encounters. By doing so, we become living testimonies to the reality and relevance of God's Kingdom in a world of competing ideologies.

The rapid advancement of technology in our era brings new dimensions to the application of Kingdom principles. While technology offers unprecedented opportunities for spreading the message of God's Kingdom and connecting believers globally, it also presents challenges such as digital addiction, the spread of misinformation, and the erosion of genuine human connection. Navigating this digital landscape with Kingdom values requires discernment, intentionality, and a commitment to using technological tools in ways that honor God and serve others.

Ultimately, living out the prayer "Thy Kingdom Come" is a daily endeavor that impacts every aspect of our lives. It influences how we make decisions, from major life choices to seemingly insignificant daily actions. It shapes our relationships, guiding us to treat others with the love, forgiveness, and grace characteristic of God's Kingdom. It informs our work ethic, encouraging us to view our vocations as opportunities to contribute to God's purposes on earth. It affects our stewardship of resources, prompting us to use our time, talents, and treasures in ways that advance Kingdom values.

As we strive to align our lives with the prayer "Thy Kingdom Come," we participate in a grand, cosmic narrative that transcends our individual existence. We become part of a global community of believers who, across cultures and generations, have longed for and worked towards the full realization of God's Kingdom on earth. This perspective imbues our daily lives with profound meaning and purpose, reminding us that even our smallest actions can contribute to the unfolding of God's grand design.

In essence, praying and living "Thy Kingdom Come" in today's world is a radical act of faith and obedience. It's a declaration that we trust in God's ultimate sovereignty and goodness, even amidst the chaos and challenges of our time. It's a commitment to be agents of transformation, allowing God to work through us to bring glimpses of His Kingdom into the here and now. As we embrace this Kingdom-minded approach to life, we not only experience personal transformation but also become catalysts for positive change in our families, communities, and the world at large.

CHAPTER 5: "GIVE US THIS DAY OUR DAILY BREAD": TRUSTING IN GOD'S PROVISION

The Meaning of "Daily Bread"

The phrase "Give us this day our daily bread" is deceptively simple, yet it carries profound depth and significance. To fully grasp its meaning, we must first unpack the linguistic and cultural nuances embedded within these few words.

At the heart of this phrase lies the mysterious Greek word "epiousios," typically translated as "daily." This term has puzzled scholars for centuries, as it appears nowhere else in ancient Greek literature outside of the Lord's Prayer. Some interpret it as "for the coming day," emphasizing a forward-looking trust in God's provision. Others understand it as "necessary for existence," focusing on the bare essentials needed for life. This linguistic ambiguity invites us to consider both our immediate needs and our ongoing reliance on God's sustenance.

In Jesus' time, bread was far more than a dietary staple; it was a symbol of life itself. For most people in ancient Near Eastern culture, bread formed the core of every meal and was often used as a utensil to scoop other foods. When Jesus taught His disciples to pray for "daily bread," He was invoking an image that resonated deeply with their everyday experience. This prayer wasn't just about food; it was a request for all that is necessary to sustain life.

Beyond its literal meaning, "bread" has long been understood in spiritual terms as well. Many Church Fathers, such as Augustine of Hippo, saw in this petition a request not just for physical nourishment, but for spiritual sustenance. They connected it to Jesus' words in John 6:35, where He declares, "I am the bread of life." In this light, praying for daily bread becomes a way of asking for Christ's presence and nourishment for our souls.

The emphasis on "daily" provision is particularly significant. It echoes God's provision of manna to the Israelites in the wilderness, where they were instructed to gather only enough for each day. This daily dependence fostered an ongoing trust in God's faithfulness. By teaching us to pray for daily bread, Jesus encourages a similar posture of daily reliance on God, countering our human tendency to anxiously hoard or independently secure our future.

This focus on daily provision also speaks to the delicate balance between material and spiritual needs. Jesus elsewhere teaches, "Man shall not live by bread alone, but by every word that comes from the mouth of God" (Matthew 4:4). By including this request for bread in a prayer otherwise focused on spiritual matters, Jesus demonstrates a holistic view of human needs. He acknowledges that we are both physical and spiritual beings, dependent on God for every aspect of our existence.

In our modern world of abundance and long-term planning, the concept of praying for daily bread might seem quaint or unnecessary. Yet, it serves as a powerful reminder of our fundamental dependence on God. Whether we live in plenty or in want, this prayer calls us to recognize the source of all we have and to trust in God's ongoing provision.

Moreover, the use of "our" rather than "my" bread points to the communal nature of this provision. It reminds us that we are part of a larger community and that our concern should extend beyond our own needs to those of others. This subtle shift in language challenges us to consider how we might participate in God's provision for our broader community.

As we contemplate the meaning of "daily bread," we are invited to examine our relationship with material possessions, our trust in God's provision, and our responsibility to our community. This simple phrase encapsulates a radical trust in God's care, a contentment with having enough, and a daily renewal of our dependence on divine grace. It calls us to live with open hands, receiving God's gifts with gratitude and sharing them with generosity.

Trusting in God's Provision

At the heart of the phrase "Give us this day our daily bread" lies a profound invitation to trust in God's provision. This simple request encapsulates a transformative approach to our relationship with the Divine and our attitude towards material needs.

Acknowledging our dependence on God is the first step in this journey of trust. By praying for daily bread, we recognize that ultimately, all we have comes from God. This act of recognition shifts our perspective from self-reliance to God-reliance, fostering a deep sense of humility and gratitude. It reminds us that our abilities, opportunities, and resources are gifts from a benevolent Creator, not solely the fruits of our own efforts.

This prayer also serves as a powerful antidote to anxiety and worry about the future. Jesus, in his Sermon on the Mount, teaches, "Do not worry about tomorrow, for tomorrow will worry about itself" (Matthew 6:34). This aligns perfectly with the prayer's focus on daily needs. By asking for what we need today, we are encouraged to release our grip on future uncertainties and trust that God will provide when the time comes. This doesn't mean we abandon planning or foresight, but rather that we hold our plans loosely, always subject to God's provision and guidance.

Contentment with sufficiency is another crucial aspect of this trust. The prayer doesn't ask for abundance or excess, but for what is sufficient for the day. This echoes the wisdom found in Proverbs 30:8, "Give me neither poverty nor riches, but give me only my daily bread." By focusing on sufficiency rather than abundance, we cultivate a spirit of contentment and gratitude. This contentment can be deeply liberating, freeing us from the endless pursuit of more and allowing us to find joy and satisfaction in what we have.

Central to this prayer is the recognition of God as the ultimate provider. This shifts our trust from our own efforts or societal systems to God's faithfulness. While we certainly play a role in meeting our needs through work and wise stewardship, this prayer reminds us that behind all our efforts stands a God who ultimately provides. This perspective can bring great peace, especially in times of scarcity or uncertainty.

Perhaps most profoundly, this daily dependence on God fosters a deeper, more intimate relationship with Him. Just as the Israelites had to trust God daily for manna in the wilderness, this prayer cultivates a daily, living relationship with God. It invites us into a rhythm of daily communion with God, where we bring our needs before Him and trust in His provision. This daily interaction can transform our spiritual lives, moving us from a distant, occasional relationship with God to one of constant, intimate trust.

In our modern world of self-reliance and material abundance, the concept of trusting God for daily provision might seem outdated or unnecessary. However, embracing this trust can bring a profound sense of peace, contentment, and spiritual connection that no amount of self-sufficiency can provide. It reminds us that regardless of our circumstances, we are ultimately dependent beings, reliant on a loving God who cares for our needs.

As we pray "Give us this day our daily bread," we are not just asking for physical sustenance, but inviting God into every aspect of our lives. We are acknowledging our dependence, releasing our anxieties, cultivating contentment, recognizing God's role as provider, and deepening our relationship with Him. This simple prayer, when embraced fully, has the power to transform not just our attitude towards material needs, but our entire approach to life and faith.

Historical and Biblical Context

The phrase "Give us this day our daily bread" is deeply rooted in the historical and biblical narrative of God's provision for His people. This section explores the rich tapestry of connections between this simple request and the broader story of faith.

The most immediate parallel in biblical history is the Exodus narrative, particularly God's provision of manna to the Israelites in the wilderness. As the newly liberated people journeyed through the desert, they faced the stark reality of potential starvation. In response to their need, God provided manna, a mysterious substance that appeared each morning with the dew. The Israelites were instructed to gather only enough for each day, with a double portion allowed on the sixth day to observe the Sabbath. This daily provision served not only to meet their physical needs but also as a profound lesson in trust and dependence on God.

The parallels between the manna narrative and Jesus' teaching on daily bread are striking. Both emphasize the daily nature of God's provision, encouraging a continual reliance on divine sustenance rather than human efforts at long-term security. This connection would not have been lost on Jesus' audience, who were well-versed in the stories of their ancestors. By echoing this foundational narrative, Jesus was inviting his followers into a similar posture of daily trust and dependence.

Jesus' teachings on provision extend beyond the Lord's Prayer. In the Sermon on the Mount, as recorded in Matthew 6:25-34, Jesus extensively addresses the issue of anxiety about material needs. He points to the birds of the air and the lilies of the field as examples of God's faithful provision, urging his listeners not to worry about tomorrow but to seek first the kingdom of God. This teaching aligns perfectly with the prayer for daily bread, reinforcing the idea that God is both willing and able to meet our daily needs.

The Old Testament is replete with similar themes of divine provision. The Psalms, in particular, often speak of God as the ultimate provider. Psalm 145:15-16 declares, "The eyes of all look to you, and you give them their food at the proper time. You open your hand and satisfy the desires of every living thing." This poetic language paints a picture of a God who is intimately involved in meeting the needs of His creation, a theme that Jesus picks up and personalizes in the Lord's Prayer.

Understanding the socio-economic context of first-century Palestine adds another layer of significance to this prayer. Many of Jesus' followers were day laborers or subsistence farmers, for whom the concern for daily provision was not a theoretical exercise but a pressing daily reality. In a society without modern social safety nets, the assurance of God's daily provision would have been a profound source of comfort and security.

The early Christian community took this teaching to heart, as evidenced in the book of Acts. The early Church practiced a radical form of communal sharing, ensuring that everyone's daily needs were met. Acts 2:44-45 describes how "All the believers were together and had everything in common. They sold property and possessions to give to anyone who had need." This practice can be seen as a practical outworking of the prayer for "our daily bread," emphasizing the communal nature of both the request and its fulfillment.

Early Church Fathers and theologians continued to reflect on the significance of this prayer. St. Augustine, for instance, saw in the request for daily bread not just a plea for physical sustenance but also for spiritual nourishment. This interpretation broadened the understanding of "bread" to include the Word of God and, for many, the Eucharist.

The historical and biblical context of "Give us this day our daily bread" reveals a rich tapestry of meaning. It connects the present-day believer to the grand narrative of God's provision throughout history, from the manna in the wilderness to the early Christian community. It reminds us that our dependence on God for daily needs is not a new concept, but one deeply woven into the fabric of faith. This context invites us to see our own requests for provision as part of this ongoing story of God's faithfulness to His people.

Psychological and Social Implications

The phrase "Give us this day our daily bread" carries profound psychological and social implications that extend far beyond its literal meaning. This simple request for daily provision has the power to shape our mental well-being, social interactions, and overall approach to life in remarkable ways.

One of the most significant psychological impacts of this prayer is on mental well-being. By focusing on daily provision rather than long-term accumulation, this mindset can significantly reduce anxiety and stress related to future uncertainties. Studies have consistently shown that practicing gratitude and cultivating trust in a higher power can lead to reduced symptoms of anxiety and depression. When individuals internalize the concept of daily provision, they may find themselves better equipped to handle the pressures of modern life, living more fully in the present moment rather than constantly worrying about future needs.

This aspect of the Lord's Prayer also fosters a sense of community interdependence. The use of "our" bread rather than "my" bread implies a collective approach to ensuring everyone's needs are met. This subtle linguistic choice encourages a shift from individualistic thinking to a more communal mindset. In practice, this can manifest as increased empathy, generosity, and social responsibility. Communities that embrace this concept might be more likely to establish support systems and safety nets for their most vulnerable members, recognizing that the well-being of each individual contributes to the health of the whole.

The prayer's emphasis on daily provision also has interesting implications for attitudes towards work and labor. It strikes a delicate balance between acknowledging the necessity of human effort and trusting in divine provision. This perspective can lead to a healthier approach to work-life balance. Instead of falling into the trap of overwork and burnout in pursuit of future security, individuals might find themselves more content with doing their best for the day at hand, trusting that tomorrow's needs will be met in turn. This doesn't negate the importance of diligence and responsibility but rather places them within a framework of trust and sufficiency.

In our modern context of rampant consumerism and materialism, the concept of 'daily bread' serves as a powerful countercultural force. It challenges the prevailing narrative that more is always better, encouraging instead a focus on sufficiency and gratitude for what we have. This shift in perspective can lead to more intentional consumption patterns, reduced waste, and a greater appreciation for the simple necessities of life. In a world where advertising constantly tells us we need more to be happy, the prayer reminds us that having enough for today is a profound blessing.

Lastly, the practice of daily reliance on a higher power for provision can build psychological resilience. By focusing on today's needs rather than anxiously planning for every possible future scenario, individuals may develop a greater capacity to adapt to unforeseen challenges. This resilience is not born of self-reliance but rather of a deep-seated trust that resources - both internal and external - will be available when needed.

The psychological and social implications of "Give us this day our daily bread" are far-reaching and transformative. From enhancing mental well-being and fostering community spirit to reshaping our approach to work and consumption, this simple prayer has the potential to radically alter how we perceive our needs and interact with the world around us. As we internalize its teachings, we may find ourselves living with greater peace, generosity, and contentment, trusting in the provision of each new day.

Contemporary Applications

In our modern world of abundance and instant gratification, the simple request for "daily bread" might seem outdated or irrelevant. However, this timeless prayer holds profound wisdom that can transform our approach to life in contemporary society.

Even in wealthy nations where food scarcity is not a primary concern, the concept of "daily bread" can shift our focus from accumulation to gratitude and sufficiency. In a culture that often equates success with excess, this prayer reminds us to appreciate what we have and find contentment in enough. It challenges the insatiable appetite for more that drives consumerism and can lead to spiritual and emotional emptiness.

This perspective can significantly influence our approach to financial planning and stewardship. Rather than anxiously hoarding wealth for an uncertain future, we might find a balance between responsible saving and generous giving. The prayer encourages us to trust in ongoing provision, potentially leading to a more open-handed approach to our resources. This could manifest in increased charitable giving, ethical investing, or simply a reduced stress level about financial matters.

On a global scale, the prayer for "our daily bread" serves as a powerful reminder of our interconnectedness and shared responsibility. In a world where hunger and poverty persist alongside abundance, this prayer can motivate action towards more equitable distribution of resources. It challenges us to see beyond our immediate circles and recognize that the bread we pray for is not just for "me" but for "us." This perspective could drive support for international aid efforts, fair trade practices, and policies that address systemic inequalities.

The concept of "daily bread" also has profound implications for environmental stewardship. In praying for provision for today, we are reminded of our dependence on the earth's resources and our responsibility to ensure their sustainability for future generations. This could inspire support for sustainable agriculture practices, reduced waste, and conservation efforts. The prayer encourages a shift from a mindset of unlimited consumption to one of responsible stewardship.

In our digital age, the application of this prayer extends beyond material needs. We might consider praying for our "daily" wisdom or discernment in navigating the constant stream of information and challenges we face. In an era of information overload and rapid technological change, the prayer reminds us to seek what we need for today, rather than being overwhelmed by the possibilities of tomorrow.

The prayer can also shape our approach to work and productivity. In a culture that often glorifies busyness and overwork, the concept of "daily bread" encourages a healthier work-life balance. It reminds us that there is virtue in doing enough for today, rather than exhausting ourselves for an uncertain future.

Lastly, in our often-individualistic society, this prayer reminds us of the importance of community. The use of "our" rather than "my" bread implies a shared responsibility for ensuring everyone's needs are met. This could manifest in supporting local food banks, engaging in community service, or simply being more attuned to the needs of our neighbors.

In conclusion, while the prayer for "daily bread" may seem simple, its applications in contemporary life are far-reaching. It challenges our assumptions about wealth, success, and security, calling us to a life of trust, gratitude, and community responsibility. As we navigate the complexities of modern life, this ancient prayer offers a grounding perspective that can lead to greater contentment, generosity, and mindful living.

Spiritual Practice and Personal Growth

The petition for daily bread in the Lord's Prayer is not merely a request for physical sustenance; it serves as a powerful tool for spiritual practice and personal growth. As we delve deeper into this aspect of the prayer, we uncover its transformative potential in our daily lives.

Cultivating daily gratitude is perhaps one of the most profound outcomes of praying for our daily bread. By acknowledging God as the source of our daily provision, we shift our focus from what we lack to what we have been given. This simple act of recognition can foster a deep sense of thankfulness that permeates all aspects of our lives. As we pray for and acknowledge our 'daily bread,' it can become a powerful gratitude practice, reminding us of God's constant care and provision. This attitude of gratitude has been shown to have numerous psychological benefits, including increased happiness, reduced stress, and improved overall well-being.

Moreover, the regular practice of praying for daily provision can significantly develop our trust in God. As we consistently bring our needs before God and witness how they are met - often in unexpected ways - our faith in God's provision grows. This isn't about testing God or treating prayer as a transactional exchange, but rather about cultivating a deeper reliance on God's faithfulness. As we pray this daily and see our needs met, our faith in God's provision can grow, leading to a more profound and intimate relationship with our Creator.

The concept of daily bread also teaches us the delicate balance between action and surrender. While we pray for God's provision, we are not called to passive inaction. Instead, this prayer encourages us to work diligently while ultimately trusting God for the results. It's a reminder that while we are called to be responsible stewards of our resources and talents, the final outcome is in God's hands. This balance can lead to a healthier approach to work and life, reducing anxiety about results while maintaining a strong work ethic.

Interestingly, the focus on 'this day' in the prayer aligns closely with contemporary mindfulness practices. By directing our attention to the present moment and today's needs, we are discouraged from excessive worry about the future or regret about the past. This prayer can serve as a Christian form of mindfulness, keeping us grounded in the present moment and attuned to God's presence and provision in our immediate circumstances.

Perhaps most profoundly, regularly praying for our daily bread can deepen our understanding of God's character. It paints a picture of God not as a distant, impersonal force, but as a loving Father who is intimately concerned with our daily needs. This perspective can transform our entire approach to prayer and our relationship with God. We begin to see God as consistently present, caring, and involved in the minutiae of our lives.

The practice of praying for daily bread also fosters humility and interdependence. It reminds us that we are not self-sufficient, but rather dependent on God and often on our community for our needs. This can lead to a greater sense of connection with others and a more compassionate approach to those in need around us.

In our modern context of abundance and instant gratification, the concept of praying for daily bread can be particularly challenging and transformative. It encourages contentment with having enough rather than always striving for more. This countercultural stance can lead to greater peace and satisfaction in life, as well as a more sustainable and generous lifestyle.

Ultimately, incorporating this understanding of 'daily bread' into our spiritual practice can lead to significant personal growth. It cultivates trust, gratitude, mindfulness, and a deeper understanding of God's nature. It challenges our tendencies towards anxiety, materialism, and self-reliance. As we internalize this aspect of the Lord's Prayer, we may find ourselves transformed - more trusting, more grateful, more present, and more aligned with God's provision and purposes in our lives.

Challenges and Critiques

As we delve deeper into the profound implications of "Give us this day our daily bread," it's important to address some of the challenges and critiques that arise when considering this part of the Lord's Prayer in various contexts.

One of the most pressing issues is how to understand and interpret this prayer in the face of unanswered petitions. In a world where hunger and poverty persist, and where individuals often face dire financial crises, the promise of daily provision can seem hollow or even cruel. How do we reconcile the faith expressed in this prayer with the harsh realities many face? It's crucial to approach this question with sensitivity and nuance, recognizing that the prayer doesn't guarantee an absence of hardship, but rather invites us into a posture of trust even amidst difficulties. This understanding can lead to a deeper, more mature faith that acknowledges the complexities of human suffering while still affirming God's care and provision.

Another challenge lies in balancing the concept of divine provision with human responsibility. Does praying for our daily bread negate the need for hard work, wise planning, or prudent financial management? This question touches on the age-old theological debate about the relationship between divine sovereignty and human free will. A balanced approach recognizes that trusting in God's provision doesn't absolve us of responsibility, but rather should motivate us to be diligent stewards of the resources we're given. The prayer, in this light, becomes not just a request for provision, but an acknowledgment of our partnership with God in meeting our needs and those of others.

It's also important to address how this part of the Lord's Prayer has sometimes been misinterpreted or misused, particularly in the context of prosperity gospel teachings. Some have expanded the concept of "daily bread" to promise material wealth or abundance, which seems contrary to the prayer's intent of fostering contentment and trust in sufficient provision. This misinterpretation can lead to disappointment and disillusionment when material prosperity doesn't materialize, potentially damaging one's faith. It's crucial to maintain the prayer's focus on daily needs rather than excessive wants, and to understand prosperity in a holistic sense that includes spiritual and relational wellbeing, not just material wealth.

The relevance and interpretation of this prayer can vary significantly across different economic contexts. In affluent societies, where basic needs are often readily met, the prayer might serve as a reminder of dependence on God and a call to gratitude and generosity. In impoverished communities, it might be understood more literally as a desperate plea for survival necessities. These varying interpretations highlight the need for a nuanced, contextual understanding of the prayer that can speak to diverse human experiences while maintaining its core spiritual truths.

Lastly, it's valuable to consider how the concept of divine provision expressed in this prayer might be viewed from interfaith perspectives. While the specific wording is distinctly Christian, the idea of trusting in divine provision is present in many faith traditions. Exploring how other religions approach this concept can enrich our understanding and foster interfaith dialogue. For instance, Islam emphasizes trust in Allah's provision (tawakkul), while Hinduism speaks of dharma, which includes the idea of cosmic provision and order. Comparing these perspectives can highlight common human needs and spiritual aspirations across different belief systems.

In grappling with these challenges and critiques, we're invited to a deeper, more mature engagement with the Lord's Prayer. Rather than seeing these issues as stumbling blocks, we can view them as opportunities for growth, fostering a faith that is robust enough to handle complexity and nuance. As we pray for our daily bread, we're called to trust deeply, think critically, act responsibly, and love compassionately, embodying the full richness of this seemingly simple request.

CHAPTER 6: "FORGIVE US OUR TRESPASSES": THE CYCLE OF DIVINE AND HUMAN FORGIVENESS

The Concept of Forgiveness in the Lord's Prayer

T he concept of forgiveness in the Lord's Prayer is a profound and multifaceted one, rooted deeply in both linguistic nuance and cultural context. To fully appreciate its significance, we must first examine the original Greek terms used in the Gospel accounts. In Matthew's version, we encounter the word "opheilēmata," which translates to "debts." Luke, on the other hand, uses "hamartias," meaning "sins." This linguistic distinction provides us with a rich tapestry of meaning to unravel.

The use of "debts" in Matthew's account is particularly illuminating when considered within the Jewish context of Jesus' time. In Jewish thought, the concept of sin was often understood through the metaphor of debt. This analogy suggests that when we sin, we incur a spiritual debt to God or to those we have wronged. By framing forgiveness in terms of debt cancellation, the prayer invokes a powerful economic metaphor that would have resonated deeply with its original audience.

Jesus' teachings on forgiveness extend far beyond the Lord's Prayer, forming a central tenet of his moral and spiritual instruction. Throughout the Gospels, we find numerous parables and direct teachings that emphasize the importance of forgiveness. The parable of the unforgiving servant in Matthew 18, for instance, dramatically illustrates the consequences of failing to extend to others the forgiveness we have received from God.

What makes the Lord's Prayer truly revolutionary is its explicit linking of divine and human forgiveness. This connection is not merely sequential but reciprocal and interdependent. The prayer suggests that our willingness to forgive others is intricately tied to our own experience of forgiveness from God. This radical proposition challenges us to view forgiveness not as an occasional act of magnanimity, but as a fundamental orientation of the heart that reflects our understanding of God's grace.

Moreover, the wording of the prayer implies that forgiveness is to be a daily practice. Just as we ask for our "daily bread," we are encouraged to engage in the ongoing work of forgiveness. This daily aspect underscores the reality that forgiveness is not a one-time event, but a continual process of releasing debts, letting go of grudges, and renewing relationships.

The concept of forgiveness presented in the Lord's Prayer thus emerges as a transformative principle, one that has the power to reshape our understanding of spirituality, morality, and community. It calls us to a higher standard of interpersonal relationships, grounded in the recognition of our own need for forgiveness and the boundless mercy of God. As we delve deeper into this prayer, we find that its teaching on forgiveness is not just a religious nicety, but a radical call to reorient our entire approach to human interaction and divine grace.

The Vertical Dimension: Divine Forgiveness

At the heart of the Lord's Prayer lies a profound truth about the nature of divine forgiveness, serving as the foundation for our understanding of human forgiveness. This vertical dimension of forgiveness—from God to humanity—sets the stage for the transformative power of grace in our lives and relationships.

God's forgiveness is not merely a theological concept but a cornerstone of the Christian faith. It is the bedrock upon which human forgiveness is built. When we pray, "Forgive us our debts," we acknowledge our need for divine mercy and grace. This recognition of our own fallenness and dependence on God's forgiveness creates the necessary humility and empathy required to extend forgiveness to others.

Central to this understanding is the concept of God as a forgiving Father. Jesus consistently portrays God not as a distant, vengeful deity, but as a loving, compassionate parent eager to reconcile with His children. This image of God as Father radically reshapes our approach to seeking forgiveness. We come not as trembling subjects before an unyielding judge, but as beloved children approaching a Parent who longs for our restoration.

However, the role of confession and repentance in seeking divine forgiveness cannot be overlooked. While God's love is unconditional, the full experience of His forgiveness often involves our active participation through honest self-reflection and a willingness to change. This process of confession —acknowledging our faults and shortcomings—is not about earning God's forgiveness but about opening ourselves fully to receive it.

Interestingly, the Lord's Prayer presents forgiveness in a communal context. We pray, "Forgive us our debts," not "Forgive me my debts." This collective approach to seeking forgiveness has profound theological implications. It suggests that our sins not only affect our individual relationship with God but also impact our community. By praying together for forgiveness, we acknowledge our shared humanity, our collective need for grace, and our interconnectedness in both sin and redemption.

Yet, this petition for forgiveness introduces a tension that has puzzled theologians for centuries. If God's love is unconditional, why does the prayer seem to make His forgiveness conditional on our forgiveness of others? This apparent paradox invites us to consider the holistic nature of God's redemptive work. Perhaps the condition is not so much about earning God's forgiveness as it is about fully realizing and embodying it. Our willingness to forgive others becomes both a sign of having truly received God's forgiveness and a means by which we more fully experience it.

Divine forgiveness, as presented in the Lord's Prayer, is not a one-time event but an ongoing reality. The present tense used in the prayer—"Forgive us"—suggests a continual process of seeking and receiving God's grace. This aligns with the Christian understanding of sanctification, where believers are continually being transformed into the likeness of Christ.

Moreover, God's forgiveness serves as a model for human forgiveness. The unlimited nature of divine forgiveness —"seventy times seven" as Jesus taught—sets a high standard for our own practice of forgiveness. It challenges us to extend grace even when it seems humanly impossible, reminding us that we too have been forgiven much.

In conclusion, the vertical dimension of forgiveness in the Lord's Prayer reveals a God who is both transcendent in His holiness and immanent in His love. It invites us into a dynamic relationship where we continually experience and extend forgiveness. This divine forgiveness not only reconciles us to God but also empowers us to be agents of reconciliation in our world, bridging the gap between the vertical and horizontal dimensions of forgiveness.

The Horizontal Dimension: Human Forgiveness

The Lord's Prayer presents a profound challenge in its call for human forgiveness, establishing it as a prerequisite for receiving divine forgiveness. This radical concept invites us to explore the transformative power of forgiveness in our relationships and communities.

At its core, the petition "forgive us our trespasses, as we forgive those who trespass against us" establishes a direct link between our willingness to forgive others and our own reception of forgiveness. This connection is not merely a suggestion but a fundamental principle of Christian spirituality. Jesus reinforces this idea in his teachings, most notably in the parable of the unforgiving servant (Matthew 18:21-35), where he illustrates the incongruity of receiving God's forgiveness while refusing to extend the same grace to others.

The psychological benefits of practicing forgiveness are well-documented. Studies have shown that individuals who cultivate a forgiving attitude experience lower levels of stress, anxiety, and depression. Forgiveness has been linked to improved cardiovascular health, better sleep quality, and stronger immune function. By releasing the burden of resentment and anger, those who forgive often report a greater sense of peace and well-being.

On a broader scale, the societal implications of a forgiveness-based ethical framework are profound. Communities that prioritize forgiveness and reconciliation over retribution tend to experience lower levels of conflict and violence. This approach has been particularly powerful in post-conflict societies, where forgiveness has played a crucial role in healing deep-seated wounds and rebuilding fractured relationships. The Truth and Reconciliation Commission in South Africa, for instance, demonstrated how forgiveness could be a cornerstone for national healing and unity.

However, it's crucial to address common misconceptions about forgiveness. Forgiveness does not necessarily equate to reconciliation or the restoration of a relationship. It doesn't mean forgetting the offense or condoning harmful behavior. Rather, forgiveness is a personal decision to release the grip of resentment and the desire for revenge. It's about freeing oneself from the emotional bondage of past hurts, whether or not the offender acknowledges their wrongdoing or seeks amends.

For those struggling with the concept of forgiveness, there are practical steps that can help cultivate a forgiving spirit. First, it's important to acknowledge the pain and allow oneself to feel the emotions associated with the hurt. Next, one can practice empathy by trying to understand the perspective of the offender, recognizing their humanity and potential struggles. Mindfulness and meditation techniques can be helpful in managing negative emotions and fostering a calm state of mind conducive to forgiveness.

Another practical approach is to start with smaller offenses and work up to more significant hurts. Keeping a forgiveness journal can help track progress and reflect on the benefits of letting go. Seeking support from trusted friends, family members, or professionals can provide guidance and encouragement throughout the process.

It's also valuable to reframe forgiveness as a gift to oneself rather than a concession to the offender. By choosing to forgive, we free ourselves from the corrosive effects of harboring resentment and anger. This shift in perspective can make the act of forgiveness more appealing and achievable.

Ultimately, the horizontal dimension of forgiveness as presented in the Lord's Prayer invites us to participate in a transformative cycle of grace. By extending forgiveness to others, we not only fulfill a spiritual mandate but also contribute to our own healing and the well-being of our communities. This challenging yet rewarding practice has the power to break cycles of harm, foster empathy, and create spaces for reconciliation and peace.

As we grapple with this dimension of the Lord's Prayer, we are called to reflect on our own experiences of being forgiven and our capacity to forgive others. In doing so, we engage in a profound spiritual exercise that has the potential to reshape our relationships, our communities, and ultimately, our world.

The Cyclical Nature of Forgiveness

Forgiveness, as presented in the Lord's Prayer, is not a linear process but a cyclical one, creating a powerful feedback loop between divine grace and human reconciliation. This cycle begins with God's forgiveness, which serves as both the model and the motivation for our own acts of forgiveness towards others.

When we experience divine forgiveness, it profoundly changes our perspective on human relationships. The overwhelming sense of liberation and renewal that comes from being forgiven by God empowers us to extend that same grace to others. This empowerment is not merely emotional but spiritual, tapping into the transformative power of God's love working through us.

As we forgive others, inspired by God's forgiveness, we create ripples of grace that extend far beyond our immediate relationships. In families, workplaces, and communities, acts of forgiveness can break long-standing cycles of resentment and retaliation. A single act of forgiveness can inspire others to do the same, creating a cascade effect that can transform entire social networks.

This cyclical nature of forgiveness is particularly powerful in breaking cycles of vengeance and retaliation. In many conflicts, both personal and societal, each party feels justified in their anger based on past wrongs. Forgiveness interrupts this cycle, creating space for healing and reconciliation. By choosing to forgive rather than retaliate, we not only free ourselves from the burden of resentment but also open the door to potentially transformative dialogue and understanding.

The Lord's Prayer encourages us to view forgiveness not as a one-time event but as a daily spiritual practice. Just as we pray for our daily bread, we are called to engage in the give-and-take of forgiveness on a regular basis. This daily practice helps to cultivate a forgiving spirit, making it easier over time to extend grace to others, even in challenging situations.

Moreover, this ongoing cycle of receiving and extending forgiveness plays a crucial role in our spiritual growth and character development. Each time we forgive, we grow in empathy, compassion, and emotional maturity. We become more aligned with the character of God, who is described in scripture as "compassionate and gracious, slow to anger, abounding in love" (Psalm 103:8).

The cyclical nature of forgiveness also reinforces our dependence on God. As we strive to forgive others, we often find ourselves falling short, leading us back to seek God's forgiveness and strength. This constant return to divine grace keeps us humble and aware of our own need for mercy, even as we extend it to others.

In essence, the cycle of forgiveness presented in the Lord's Prayer is a powerful mechanism for personal and social transformation. It connects our vertical relationship with God to our horizontal relationships with others, creating a dynamic interplay of grace that has the potential to revolutionize our lives and our world. As we participate in this divine-human cycle of forgiveness, we become active participants in God's redemptive work, bringing healing and reconciliation to a fractured world.

Forgiveness in Various Christian Traditions

The concept of forgiveness, while central to Christianity as a whole, is interpreted and practiced differently across various Christian traditions. This diversity in approach reflects the rich tapestry of Christian thought and practice that has evolved over two millennia.

In the Catholic tradition, forgiveness is intimately tied to the sacrament of reconciliation, also known as confession. This sacramental practice involves the confession of sins to a priest, who acts as a mediator of God's forgiveness. The penitent expresses contrition, receives absolution, and is often given a penance to perform. This formal structure emphasizes the Church's role in the forgiveness process and underscores the belief that Christ gave the apostles, and by extension the Church, the power to forgive sins in His name.

Protestant views on forgiveness, shaped by the Reformation's emphasis on sola scriptura and sola fide, tend to focus more on the direct relationship between the individual and God. Many Protestant denominations teach that forgiveness is received through faith alone, without the necessity of intermediary rituals or clerical absolution. This approach often emphasizes personal prayer and Bible study as means of seeking and receiving God's forgiveness. Some Protestant traditions, particularly those influenced by Calvinism, also stress the concept of total depravity and the sufficiency of Christ's atonement, viewing forgiveness as an act of divine grace rather than something earned through human effort.

Orthodox Christian approaches to forgiveness blend liturgical practice with personal spiritual disciplines. The Orthodox Church places great emphasis on the concept of theosis, or becoming like God, in which forgiveness plays a crucial role. The practice of regular confession to a spiritual father is common, though it differs from the Catholic sacrament in its less formal nature. The Orthodox tradition also highlights communal aspects of forgiveness, particularly in the beautiful ritual of mutual forgiveness that takes place at the beginning of Great Lent.

Anabaptist and peace church traditions, including Mennonites and Quakers, place a strong emphasis on forgiveness as a cornerstone of their nonviolent ethic. These traditions often interpret Jesus' teachings on forgiveness, including those in the Lord's Prayer, as a call to radical peacemaking and reconciliation. For many in these traditions, forgiveness is not just a personal spiritual practice but a powerful tool for social transformation and conflict resolution.

Modern evangelical interpretations of forgiveness often blend elements from various Protestant traditions while emphasizing personal relationship with Jesus Christ. Many evangelical churches teach that forgiveness is received through accepting Christ as one's personal savior and is maintained through ongoing confession and repentance. There's often a strong focus on the transformative power of forgiveness in one's life and relationships.

Despite these differences, all Christian traditions recognize the centrality of forgiveness to the faith. They all draw inspiration from the same source - Christ's teaching and example - even as they interpret and apply these teachings in diverse ways. This diversity serves as a reminder of the multifaceted nature of forgiveness itself, which can be understood as a divine gift, a human choice, a spiritual discipline, and a tool for personal and social transformation.

The varying approaches to forgiveness across Christian traditions also highlight the ongoing dialogue within Christianity about how best to understand and practice this crucial aspect of faith. While these differences can sometimes lead to disagreement, they also provide a rich resource for Christians seeking to deepen their understanding and practice of forgiveness. By examining how different traditions approach forgiveness, believers can gain new insights into this fundamental aspect of their faith and potentially enrich their own spiritual practices.

Ultimately, the diversity of approaches to forgiveness in Christian traditions underscores its profound importance in Christian theology and practice. Whether through formal sacraments, personal prayer, communal rituals, or social action, the pursuit of forgiveness remains a central pillar of Christian life, reflecting the divine forgiveness exemplified by Christ and echoed in the words of the Lord's Prayer.

Forgiveness in Contemporary Context

In our modern world, the concept of forgiveness as presented in the Lord's Prayer takes on new dimensions and faces unique challenges. This ancient spiritual practice finds itself navigating the complexities of a globalized, digital, and often deeply divided society.

One of the most profound applications of forgiveness in our contemporary context is in the realm of grave injustices and atrocities. The 20th century, often called the bloodiest in human history, left in its wake numerous instances of genocide, war crimes, and systematic oppression. In response, we've seen remarkable examples of forgiveness that have captured the world's attention. The Truth and Reconciliation Commission in post-apartheid South Africa, led by Archbishop Desmond Tutu, demonstrated how forgiveness could be a powerful tool for national healing. Similarly, the Amish community's forgiveness of the gunman who killed five of their children in a 2006 school shooting in Pennsylvania showcased the transformative power of this spiritual practice on a communal level.

Forgiveness has also emerged as a crucial element in conflict resolution and peace-building efforts worldwide. International organizations and peace negotiators increasingly recognize that sustainable peace often requires more than just political agreements – it necessitates a process of forgiveness and reconciliation. The Good Friday Agreement in Northern Ireland, for instance, while primarily a political settlement, was underpinned by a societal shift towards forgiveness and reconciliation between communities that had been locked in conflict for generations.

Recent psychological research has shed light on the numerous health benefits associated with forgiveness. Studies have shown that individuals who practice forgiveness experience lower levels of stress, anxiety, and depression. They also tend to have better cardiovascular health and stronger immune systems. This scientific validation of the benefits of forgiveness adds a new dimension to our understanding of this spiritual practice, suggesting that the wisdom embedded in the Lord's Prayer has tangible physical and mental health implications.

The digital age has presented new challenges and opportunities for the practice of forgiveness. Cyberbullying, online harassment, and the rapid spread of misinformation have created new contexts where forgiveness is needed. The anonymity and distance provided by digital platforms can sometimes make forgiveness more difficult, as face-to-face reconciliation is not always possible. However, these same platforms also provide opportunities for widespread movements of forgiveness and reconciliation, allowing stories of forgiveness to reach and inspire millions.

Finally, the principles of forgiveness are finding application in corporate and political spheres. Some companies are incorporating forgiveness into their organizational culture, recognizing its potential to improve workplace relationships, increase productivity, and reduce employee turnover. In politics, we've seen instances where public figures have sought forgiveness for past actions or statements, often with mixed public reactions. These examples highlight the complex interplay between personal forgiveness, public accountability, and societal expectations.

As we navigate these contemporary contexts, the forgiveness petition in the Lord's Prayer continues to challenge and inspire us. It reminds us that forgiveness is not just a personal spiritual practice, but a powerful force that can shape our communities, our societies, and our world. In a time of increasing polarization and conflict, the call to forgive as we have been forgiven offers a radical alternative – a path towards healing, reconciliation, and renewed relationships. As we grapple with the complexities of forgiveness in our modern world, we find that this ancient prayer speaks with renewed relevance and urgency to our contemporary challenges.

Challenges and Criticisms of the Forgiveness Mandate

While the forgiveness component of the Lord's Prayer has been a cornerstone of Christian theology and practice for centuries, it is not without its critics and challenges. This section explores some of the key concerns and criticisms raised about the forgiveness mandate, offering a balanced perspective on this complex issue.

One of the primary theological critiques of the forgiveness clause in the Lord's Prayer centers on its seemingly conditional nature. Some scholars argue that the implication that God's forgiveness is contingent upon our forgiveness of others appears to contradict the concept of God's unconditional love and grace. This apparent conditionality has led to debates about the nature of divine forgiveness and whether human actions can truly influence God's willingness to forgive.

From a psychological standpoint, concerns have been raised about the potential misuse or abuse of forgiveness rhetoric. In situations of ongoing abuse or injustice, an overemphasis on forgiveness could potentially lead to victims feeling pressured to forgive prematurely or to remain in harmful situations. Mental health professionals caution that while forgiveness can be healing, it should not come at the expense of personal safety or justice.

Feminist and liberation theology perspectives have also contributed valuable critiques to the discourse on forgiveness. These theological approaches often emphasize the importance of addressing systemic injustices and power imbalances alongside personal forgiveness. They argue that a simplistic understanding of forgiveness could potentially perpetuate oppressive structures by encouraging the oppressed to forgive without addressing the root causes of injustice.

Perhaps one of the most profound challenges to the forgiveness mandate is the question of forgiving the "unforgivable." In the face of extreme atrocities, genocide, or deeply personal betrayals, the call to forgive can seem not only difficult but morally questionable. This challenge raises important questions about the limits of human forgiveness and how to reconcile the Christian ideal of forgiveness with the reality of human suffering and the need for justice.

Balancing justice and forgiveness in both personal and societal contexts presents another significant challenge. While forgiveness is often presented as a virtue, there are legitimate concerns about how it intersects with the need for accountability and restitution. In legal and political spheres, questions arise about how to implement forgiveness-based approaches without undermining the rule of law or the pursuit of justice.

It's also worth noting that the interpretation and application of the forgiveness mandate can vary significantly across different cultural contexts. What might be considered forgivable in one culture could be viewed as unforgivable in another, highlighting the need for nuanced, culturally-sensitive approaches to understanding and practicing forgiveness.

Despite these challenges and criticisms, many theologians

and practitioners argue that the forgiveness mandate in the Lord's Prayer remains a profound and transformative teaching. They suggest that a deeper, more nuanced understanding of forgiveness—one that doesn't negate justice or ignore the complexity of human relationships—can address many of these concerns.

Ultimately, the challenges to the forgiveness mandate serve an important purpose in pushing believers to grapple with the complexities of forgiveness in real-world situations. They encourage a more thoughtful, nuanced approach to forgiveness that takes into account psychological, social, and justice considerations alongside spiritual ones.

As we continue to wrestle with these challenges, it becomes clear that the forgiveness component of the Lord's Prayer is not a simple, one-size-fits-all command, but rather an invitation to engage deeply with one of the most profound and transformative practices in human experience. It calls us to continually reflect on what it means to forgive, to be forgiven, and to live in a world where both divine and human forgiveness play crucial roles in our personal and collective well-being.

CHAPTER 7: "LEAD US NOT INTO TEMPTATION": SPIRITUAL WARFARE AND DIVINE PROTECTION

Understanding Temptation in Biblical Context

To fully grasp the significance of the phrase "Lead us not into temptation" in the Lord's Prayer, we must first understand the concept of temptation as it is presented in biblical context. In the Christian tradition, temptation is more than just a fleeting desire or a momentary urge to do something wrong. It is a profound spiritual challenge that tests one's faith, character, and commitment to God.

The Greek word used in the New Testament for temptation is "peirasmos," which carries a broader meaning than our modern English understanding. This term encompasses not only the enticement to sin but also trials, tests, and ordeals that can potentially lead one astray from their faith. This nuanced interpretation adds depth to our understanding of what Jesus meant when He taught His disciples to pray for protection against temptation.

Perhaps the most illustrative example of temptation in the Bible is Jesus' own experience in the wilderness. After His baptism, Jesus was led by the Spirit into the desert, where He fasted for forty days and nights. During this time of physical weakness, He faced three distinct temptations from Satan. This account serves as a model for believers, demonstrating that even the Son of God faced temptation and providing insight into how one can resist such challenges.

In each instance of temptation, Jesus responded with scripture, showcasing the power of God's Word as a defense against spiritual attacks. This episode highlights an essential aspect of temptation: the role of free will. Despite the intensity of the temptations and His physical vulnerability, Jesus chose to resist. This underscores the Christian belief that while temptation itself is not sin, yielding to it is a matter of personal choice.

It's crucial to distinguish between temptation and testing in scripture. While both involve challenges to one's faith, their sources and purposes differ. Temptation, often attributed to Satan or one's own sinful nature, aims to lead individuals away from God. Testing, on the other hand, can come from God Himself, not to lead one into sin, but to strengthen faith and character. The book of James makes this distinction clear: "When tempted, no one should say, 'God is tempting me.' For God cannot be tempted by evil, nor does he tempt anyone" (James 1:13).

Understanding temptation in its biblical context reveals its complexity and significance in the spiritual life of believers. It's not merely about avoiding wrongdoing, but about maintaining steadfast faith in the face of spiritual challenges. When we pray, "Lead us not into temptation," we are acknowledging our vulnerability to these spiritual trials and our dependence on God's guidance and protection. This petition is a humble admission of our human frailty and a powerful invocation of divine strength in our daily spiritual battles.

The Reality of Spiritual Warfare

The concept of spiritual warfare is deeply rooted in Christian theology, representing an ongoing battle between good and evil that extends beyond the physical realm. This spiritual conflict, while often invisible to the naked eye, is believed to have profound implications for the lives of believers and the world at large.

To understand spiritual warfare, we must first examine its biblical foundations. Throughout scripture, we find numerous references to spiritual battles. In the Old Testament, we see glimpses of this conflict in stories like Job's trials and Daniel's visions. The New Testament, however, provides a more explicit framework for understanding spiritual warfare. The Apostle Paul, in his letter to the Ephesians, famously writes, "For our struggle is not against flesh and blood, but against the rulers, against the authorities, against the powers of this dark world and against the spiritual forces of evil in the heavenly realms" (Ephesians 6:12). This passage encapsulates the essence of spiritual warfare, highlighting the unseen nature of the battle and the formidable opponents believers face.

Central to the concept of spiritual warfare is the nature of evil itself. Christian theology has long grappled with whether to view evil as a personal force, embodied in figures like Satan, or as an impersonal force of darkness and corruption. Many traditions embrace a hybrid view, recognizing both personal spiritual entities and systemic evils that permeate societies and institutions. This nuanced understanding allows for a comprehensive approach to addressing evil in its various manifestations.

In contemporary Christian thought, the understanding of spiritual warfare has evolved, influenced by advances in psychology, sociology, and other disciplines. Many modern theologians and pastors emphasize the psychological and social aspects of spiritual warfare, viewing it not just as a battle against external demonic forces, but also as an internal struggle against sinful tendencies and societal pressures that lead individuals away from God.

This more holistic approach to spiritual warfare recognizes that the battleground often lies within the human heart and mind. Temptations, doubts, fears, and negative thought patterns are seen as potential weapons of the enemy, requiring spiritual discernment and resistance. At the same time, this perspective doesn't negate the possibility of more overt spiritual attacks or demonic influence, maintaining a balance between psychological and supernatural explanations.

It's important to acknowledge that the concept of spiritual warfare is not without its skeptics, both within and outside the Christian faith. Critics argue that attributing life's challenges to spiritual forces can lead to a simplistic worldview that ignores complex social, psychological, and biological factors. Others express concern that an overemphasis on spiritual warfare can breed paranoia or a unhealthy fixation on demonic influences.

In response to these concerns, many contemporary Christian leaders advocate for a balanced approach to spiritual warfare. This perspective recognizes the reality of spiritual conflict while also affirming the importance of addressing practical, tangible issues in one's life and society. It encourages believers to be aware of spiritual realities without becoming obsessed or paralyzed by fear.

Ultimately, the concept of spiritual warfare in Christian theology serves as a reminder of the cosmic significance of human choices and actions. It frames the Christian life as one of active participation in God's redemptive work, calling believers to be vigilant, prayerful, and engaged in the ongoing struggle against evil in all its forms. Whether viewed through a more traditional lens of battling demonic forces or a more modern perspective of resisting negative influences, the essence of spiritual warfare remains a crucial element of Christian faith and practice.

As we consider the phrase "Lead us not into temptation, but deliver us from evil" in the Lord's Prayer, we see it as more than a simple request for protection. It is an acknowledgment of the spiritual battle that surrounds us and a plea for divine guidance and strength in the face of these challenges. This recognition of spiritual warfare adds depth and urgency to our prayers, reminding us of our dependence on God in navigating the complex spiritual landscape of our lives.

Divine Protection and Guidance

The concept of divine protection and guidance is a cornerstone of Christian faith, deeply rooted in scripture and theological tradition. Throughout the Bible, God is consistently portrayed as a protector, a shield, and a guide for His people. This image of God as a protector is not merely metaphorical; it reflects a profound spiritual reality that believers have relied upon for millennia.

In the Old Testament, we see numerous examples of God's protection, from His deliverance of the Israelites from Egypt to His preservation of Daniel in the lion's den. The Psalms, in particular, are replete with affirmations of God's protective nature. Psalm 91:1-2 beautifully encapsulates this trust: "Whoever dwells in the shelter of the Most High will rest in the shadow of the Almighty. I will say of the Lord, 'He is my refuge and my fortress, my God, in whom I trust.'"

In the New Testament, this concept of divine protection is further enriched by the role of the Holy Spirit. Jesus promised His disciples that the Holy Spirit would be their guide and comforter, leading them into all truth (John 16:13). This guidance is not just about imparting knowledge, but also about providing spiritual protection and discernment in the face of temptation and spiritual warfare.

However, it's crucial to understand that divine protection and guidance do not negate human responsibility. There's a delicate balance between trusting in God's protection and exercising our own free will and judgment. The apostle Paul captures this tension in Philippians 2:12-13, urging believers to "work out your own salvation with fear and trembling, for it is God who works in you, both to will and to work for his good pleasure."

This balance is further reflected in the biblical promises of protection. While scripture is filled with assurances of God's protective care, these promises are often conditional, requiring faith, obedience, and righteous living on the part of the believer. For instance, James 4:7 instructs, "Submit yourselves, then, to God. Resist the devil, and he will flee from you." Here, we see both divine protection and human responsibility working in tandem.

A common question that arises in discussions of divine protection is why believers still face temptation and trials if God is protecting them. This query touches on the heart of Christian theology regarding the nature of faith, free will, and spiritual growth. The Bible never promises a life free from temptation or hardship for believers. Instead, it assures us of God's presence and strength in the midst of these challenges.

The apostle Paul's experience, as described in 2 Corinthians 12:7-9, provides insight into this paradox. Despite his pleas for relief from his "thorn in the flesh," God's response was, "My grace is sufficient for you, for my power is made perfect in weakness." This passage suggests that sometimes, divine protection manifests not in the removal of trials, but in the provision of strength to endure them.

Moreover, the experience of temptation and trial can serve a purpose in the believer's spiritual development. James 1:2-4 encourages believers to "count it all joy" when they face trials, as these tests of faith produce perseverance and spiritual maturity. In this light, God's protection and guidance can be seen as operating on a higher plane, focused on our ultimate spiritual well-being rather than mere temporal comfort.

Understanding divine protection and guidance in this nuanced way adds depth to our interpretation of the phrase "Lead us not into temptation, but deliver us from evil" in the Lord's Prayer. It becomes clear that this is not a plea for a life devoid of challenges, but rather a recognition of our dependence on God's guidance and protection as we navigate the complexities of spiritual warfare.

In conclusion, divine protection and guidance are central themes in Christian spirituality, offering comfort and strength to believers facing life's challenges. However, this protection is not a passive shield, but an active partnership between divine grace and human faith. As we pray for God's protection and guidance, we are called to actively participate in our spiritual journey, trusting in God's wisdom and strength while exercising our own discernment and faith.

Strategies for Resisting Temptation

In our journey through life, we inevitably encounter temptations that challenge our faith and moral convictions. Developing effective strategies to resist these temptations is crucial for spiritual growth and maintaining a strong relationship with God. This section explores practical approaches to overcoming temptation, drawing inspiration from biblical teachings and contemporary wisdom.

Self-awareness is the foundation of resisting temptation. By understanding our own vulnerabilities and recognizing the situations that may lead us astray, we can better prepare ourselves to face challenges. This involves honest self reflection and a willingness to confront our weaknesses. As the apostle

Paul advises in 1 Corinthians 10:12, "So, if you think you are standing firm, be careful that you don't fall!" This reminder emphasizes the importance of remaining vigilant and aware of our susceptibilities.

Spiritual disciplines play a vital role in strengthening our resistance to temptation. Regular prayer, meditation on scripture, and fasting are powerful tools that help fortify our spiritual defenses. These practices not only deepen our relationship with God but also sharpen our discernment, enabling us to recognize and resist temptation more effectively. As Jesus demonstrated during His temptation in the wilderness, quoting scripture can be a powerful defense against the allure of sin.

The role of community in overcoming temptation cannot be overstated. Surrounding ourselves with fellow believers who can offer support, accountability, and encouragement is invaluable. The book of Hebrews emphasizes this, stating, "Let us consider how we may spur one another on toward love and good deeds, not giving up meeting together, as some are in the habit of doing, but encouraging one another" (Hebrews 10:24-25). When we share our struggles with trusted friends or mentors, we not only gain support but also break the isolation that often accompanies temptation.

Jesus' methods of dealing with temptation provide a perfect model for us to emulate. During His temptation in the wilderness, Jesus consistently responded to Satan's offers by quoting scripture. This demonstrates the power of knowing and internalizing God's Word as a defense against temptation. Additionally, Jesus often withdrew to solitary places to pray, highlighting the importance of maintaining a strong connection with the Father as a source of strength and guidance.

Prayer is perhaps the most potent tool in resisting temptation. Jesus Himself taught His disciples to pray, "Lead us not into temptation, but deliver us from evil." This prayer acknowledges our dependence on God's guidance and protection. When we face temptation, turning to God in prayer allows us to tap into His strength and wisdom. As the letter of James advises, "Submit yourselves, then, to God. Resist the devil, and he will flee from you" (James 4:7).

Practical strategies for resisting temptation also include avoiding situations that we know are likely to lead us astray. This might mean changing our routines, being mindful of the media we consume, or being selective about the company we keep. The Proverbs wisely counsel, "Above all else, guard your heart, for everything you do flows from it" (Proverbs 4:23).

It's important to remember that resisting temptation is not about achieving perfection, but about progress and growth in our faith journey. We will face setbacks and failures, but these can become opportunities for learning and renewed commitment. The apostle Paul reminds us, "No temptation has overtaken you except what is common to mankind. And God is faithful; he will not let you be tempted beyond what you can bear. But when you are tempted, he will also provide a way out so that you can endure it" (1 Corinthians 10:13).

In conclusion, resisting temptation requires a multifaceted approach that combines self-awareness, spiritual disciplines, community support, and a deep reliance on God's guidance and strength. By implementing these strategies and continually seeking God's help through prayer, we can grow stronger in our faith and more resilient in the face of life's many temptations. As we pray "Lead us not into temptation," we acknowledge our need for divine assistance and commit ourselves to the ongoing process of spiritual growth and transformation.

Delivery from Evil

The concept of "delivery from evil" is a profound and multifaceted aspect of the Lord's Prayer, carrying deep theological and practical implications for believers. In the

99

context of this prayer, "evil" encompasses a broad spectrum of negative forces that can harm, mislead, or separate us from God's love and purpose.

The Greek word used in the original text, "poneros," can be translated as both "evil" and "the evil one," suggesting that this petition addresses not only abstract notions of wickedness but also the personified force of evil often identified as Satan in Christian theology. This dual meaning invites us to consider both the systemic evils present in our world and the personal spiritual battles we face.

Deliverance, in Christian theology, is more than just rescue or protection. It implies a transformative process through which God not only shields us from harm but also empowers us to overcome evil influences in our lives. This concept is deeply rooted in the biblical narrative, from the Exodus story of God delivering the Israelites from slavery in Egypt to the New Testament's portrayal of Christ's victory over sin and death.

Faith plays a crucial role in this process of deliverance. It's not merely about believing that God can deliver us, but actively trusting in His power and goodness even in the face of evil. This faith is not passive; it requires our participation and cooperation with God's grace. As the Apostle James writes, "Resist the devil, and he will flee from you. Come near to God and he will come near to you" (James 4:7-8).

Throughout scripture, we find numerous examples of God's deliverance from evil. The story of Daniel in the lion's den, David's victories over his enemies, and Paul's endurance through persecution all illustrate God's power to protect and deliver His people. These accounts serve not only as historical testimonies but also as encouragements for believers facing their own battles against evil.

However, the persistence of evil in the world often raises challenging questions for believers. If God is all-powerful and loving, why does evil continue to exist? This age-old theological dilemma, often referred to as the problem of evil, has no easy answers. Yet, the Lord's Prayer doesn't shy away from this reality. Instead, it acknowledges the presence of evil while affirming God's ultimate authority and our dependence on Him.

The petition for delivery from evil is not a guarantee of a trouble-free life, but rather a recognition of our need for God's guidance and protection in navigating a world where evil exists. It's a humble admission of our vulnerability and a bold declaration of our trust in God's power and goodness.

Moreover, this part of the prayer reminds us of our role in resisting evil. While we rely on God's deliverance, we are also called to be active participants in opposing evil in all its forms – whether personal temptations, social injustices, or systemic wickedness.

In praying for deliverance from evil, we align ourselves with God's ultimate plan for creation – the final defeat of all evil and the establishment of His kingdom in fullness. This eschatological hope gives us courage and perseverance in our present struggles, knowing that our current battles against evil are part of a larger cosmic narrative that ends in God's victory.

Ultimately, the petition "deliver us from evil" is a profound expression of trust in God's power, a realistic acknowledgment of the challenges we face, and a hopeful anticipation of God's final triumph over all forms of evil. It invites us to live with both vigilance against evil and confidence in God's deliverance, shaping our daily actions and our eternal perspective.

Contemporary Applications

In our modern world, the plea "Lead us not into temptation, but deliver us from evil" resonates with renewed significance. Today's temptations often take on different forms than those faced by our ancestors, yet they remain just as potent and pervasive. The digital age has ushered in a new era of challenges, from the constant lure of social media to the accessibility of inappropriate content online. These modern temptations can be subtle, weaving themselves into the fabric of our daily lives in ways that make them difficult to recognize and resist.

The internet and smartphones, while offering unprecedented connectivity and access to information, have also become sources of anxiety and addiction for many. The fear of missing out (FOMO) drives compulsive checking of notifications, while the curated lives presented on social media can fuel envy and discontent. In this context, praying "Lead us not into temptation" takes on new meaning, as we seek divine guidance to navigate these digital pitfalls and maintain healthy boundaries with technology.

Interestingly, the concept of spiritual warfare, once viewed primarily through a religious lens, has found relevance in secular contexts as well. Many people, regardless of their faith background, resonate with the idea of battling internal and external forces that threaten their well-being and integrity. This universal struggle against temptation and negative influences has been recognized in fields such as psychology and addiction recovery, where strategies for resistance often mirror spiritual practices.

From a psychological perspective, the act of acknowledging our vulnerability to temptation and seeking protection aligns with cognitive behavioral approaches to managing impulses and negative thoughts. The prayer can be seen as a form of mindfulness, promoting self-awareness and intentional decision-making. It encourages individuals to pause and consider their actions, rather than reacting impulsively to stimuli or desires.

Moreover, this portion of the Lord's Prayer can serve as a powerful tool in shaping ethical decision-making. In a world where moral boundaries often seem blurred, the simple act of praying for guidance and protection can help individuals clarify their values and strengthen their resolve to act in accordance with those values. It reminds us to consider the long-term consequences of our actions and to seek a higher standard in our behavior.

The prayer's emphasis on divine protection also speaks to the deep-seated human need for security in an often chaotic and unpredictable world. In an age where global threats such as climate change, political instability, and pandemics loom large, the assurance of a higher power's protection can provide comfort and resilience. It encourages a perspective that looks beyond immediate circumstances to a broader, more hopeful outlook.

Ultimately, the contemporary application of "Lead us not into temptation, but deliver us from evil" invites us to cultivate a life of intentionality and mindfulness. It challenges us to be aware of the subtle temptations and negative influences in our modern world, to seek wisdom in navigating them, and to trust in a power greater than ourselves for guidance and protection. In doing so, it offers a timeless remedy to the timely challenges of our age, proving that ancient wisdom can indeed speak powerfully to contemporary needs.

Integrating this Petition into Daily Life

The final petition of the Lord's Prayer, "Lead us not into temptation, but deliver us from evil," is not merely a set of words to be recited, but a powerful tool for spiritual growth and daily living. Incorporating this prayer into our daily routines can have a profound impact on our lives, shaping our worldview, personal growth, relationships, and long-term spiritual development.

One practical way to integrate this petition into daily life is to begin each morning by consciously reflecting on it. As we start our day, we can take a moment to acknowledge our vulnerabilities and the potential challenges we may face. By doing so, we cultivate a mindset of humility and dependence on God, recognizing our need for divine guidance and protection throughout the day.

This simple act of prayer can significantly shape our worldview. It reminds us that we are not alone in our struggles, but part of a larger spiritual reality. This perspective can provide comfort and strength, especially when facing difficult decisions or moral dilemmas. By regularly praying for guidance away from temptation and deliverance from evil, we develop a heightened awareness of the spiritual dimensions of our choices and actions.

The impact of this prayer on personal growth and character development cannot be overstated. As we consistently seek God's guidance and protection, we become more attuned to our own weaknesses and the areas where we need to grow. This self-awareness, combined with a reliance on divine assistance, can lead to significant personal transformation over time. We may find ourselves becoming more resilient in the face of temptation, more discerning in our choices, and more aligned with our spiritual values.

Moreover, this petition can profoundly influence our interpersonal relationships. As we become more aware of our own need for guidance and protection, we often develop greater empathy for others facing similar struggles. This can lead to more compassionate and understanding relationships. Additionally, by acknowledging the reality of evil and the need for deliverance, we may become more forgiving of others' shortcomings and more proactive in supporting those around us in their spiritual journeys.

The long-term effects of consistently praying this petition are far-reaching. Over time, it can lead to a deeper sense of trust in God's providence and a greater awareness of His presence in our daily lives. This sustained practice can result in a more peaceful and contented outlook, even in the face of life's challenges. We may find ourselves better equipped to navigate the complexities of modern life, with a stronger moral compass and a clearer sense of purpose.

Furthermore, regularly engaging with this part of the Lord's Prayer can foster a community of believers who support and encourage one another in their spiritual growth. As we share our experiences of temptation, deliverance, and divine protection, we create a network of mutual support and accountability.

In conclusion, integrating "Lead us not into temptation, but deliver us from evil" into our daily lives is a transformative practice. It's not just about avoiding wrong or seeking protection; it's about actively aligning our lives with God's will and growing in spiritual maturity. This simple yet profound petition has the power to shape our character, influence our decisions, improve our relationships, and deepen our faith. As we make this prayer a consistent part of our daily routine, we open ourselves to the guidance and protection of a loving God, finding strength and courage to face whatever challenges life may bring.

CHAPTER 8: THE LORD'S PRAYER IN JEWISH AND EARLY CHRISTIAN TRADITION

Jewish Roots of the Lord's Prayer

The Lord's Prayer, a cornerstone of Christian worship, is deeply rooted in Jewish tradition. This connection is not merely superficial but reaches into the very heart of Jewish spiritual practices and theological concepts. To fully appreciate the Lord's Prayer, we must first understand its Jewish foundations.

One of the most striking similarities is found between the Lord's Prayer and the Kaddish, an ancient Jewish prayer still recited in synagogues today. Both prayers begin by sanctifying God's name and expressing hope for the establishment of God's kingdom. This parallel underscores the continuity between Jewish and early Christian worship practices, revealing how Jesus and his followers were firmly grounded in their Jewish heritage.

The structure of the Lord's Prayer also reflects patterns common in synagogue worship of the first century. Jewish prayers often followed a similar format, beginning with praise to God, followed by petitions, and concluding with further praise or affirmation. This structure, familiar to Jesus' Jewish audience, provided a comforting and recognizable framework for the revolutionary content of his teaching.

Furthermore, the Lord's Prayer incorporates several key concepts central to Jewish theology. The ideas of God's kingdom, daily provision, and forgiveness of sins were all familiar themes in Jewish thought. By weaving these concepts into his prayer, Jesus was not introducing entirely new ideas but rather reframing and reinterpreting existing Jewish beliefs in light of his own mission and message.

Elements of the Lord's Prayer can also be traced back to prayers found in the Hebrew Bible. For instance, the plea for daily bread echoes the Israelites' dependence on manna in the wilderness, while the request for forgiveness resonates with numerous psalms and prophetic writings. These connections demonstrate how Jesus was not breaking with Jewish tradition but building upon it, offering a new perspective on ancient truths.

Perhaps the most revolutionary aspect of the Lord's Prayer in its Jewish context is the intimate form of address to God as "Father." While the concept of God as a father figure was not entirely foreign to Jewish thought, the direct and personal way Jesus encouraged his followers to address God was unprecedented. This shift in perspective invited believers into a more intimate relationship with the Divine, challenging traditional notions of God's transcendence and distance.

The Jewish roots of the Lord's Prayer reveal a profound continuity between the Old and New Testaments, between the faith of Israel and the emerging Christian movement. Far from being a complete departure from Jewish tradition, the Lord's Prayer represents a reinterpretation and fulfillment of Jewish spiritual ideals. It stands as a testament to Jesus' role not as the founder of an entirely new religion, but as a Jewish teacher offering a radical new understanding of his people's ancient faith.

The Lord's Prayer in its Historical Setting

The Lord's Prayer emerged during a tumultuous period in Jewish history, specifically in first-century Palestine under Roman occupation. This historical context profoundly shaped the prayer's content and significance for early Christians.

At the time of Jesus, Palestine was a province of the Roman Empire, governed by prefects appointed by Rome. The Jewish population chafed under foreign rule, longing for liberation and the restoration of their national sovereignty. This political climate fostered a period of intense messianic expectation, with many Jews eagerly anticipating a divinely appointed leader who would overthrow their oppressors and usher in God's kingdom on earth.

Within this charged atmosphere, various Jewish religious movements flourished, each offering its own interpretation of how to live faithfully under foreign domination. The Pharisees advocated strict adherence to the Law, while the Sadducees collaborated with Roman authorities to maintain their privileged position. The Essenes withdrew from society to pursue ritual purity, and the Zealots actively resisted Roman rule through violent means. Jesus' teachings, including the Lord's Prayer, emerged as a distinct voice amidst these competing ideologies.

The prayer's historical setting was further complicated by the pervasive influence of Greek and Roman culture throughout the Mediterranean world. This Hellenistic influence had been reshaping Jewish thought and practice for centuries, leading to a complex interplay between traditional Jewish beliefs and broader philosophical and religious ideas of the time.

It was in this context of growing tension with religious

authorities that Jesus taught the Lord's Prayer to his disciples. His emphasis on addressing God as "Father" and petitioning for the coming of God's kingdom resonated deeply with the messianic hopes of his contemporaries. However, Jesus' interpretation of these concepts often challenged prevailing assumptions, as seen in his teachings on non-violent resistance and love for enemies.

The prayer's request for "daily bread" took on particular significance in a society where many lived on the edge of subsistence, vulnerable to the whims of nature and political instability. Similarly, the plea for forgiveness of debts echoed the economic realities of an agrarian society burdened by heavy taxation and indebtedness.

The final petitions regarding temptation and deliverance from evil reflected the spiritual struggles of a people living under oppression, torn between accommodation to Roman rule and the desire for divine intervention. These themes would have resonated powerfully with Jesus' initial audience, who were navigating the complex realities of life under foreign domination while holding fast to their faith in God's ultimate sovereignty.

Understanding this historical setting enriches our appreciation of the Lord's Prayer. Far from being a timeless, abstract formula, it was deeply rooted in the lived experiences and spiritual yearnings of first-century Palestinian Jews. As we continue to pray these words today, we connect not only with a sacred tradition but with the hopes, fears, and faith of those who first uttered them in a world both vastly different from and surprisingly similar to our own.

Gospel Accounts of the Lord's Prayer

The Lord's Prayer appears in two distinct versions within the Gospels, each offering unique insights into its early transmission and significance. In Matthew's Gospel, the prayer is presented as part of Jesus' famous Sermon on the Mount, a comprehensive teaching on righteous living and the nature of God's Kingdom. Here, the prayer serves as a model for ideal communication with God, emphasizing simplicity and sincerity over ostentatious displays of piety.

Luke's Gospel, on the other hand, introduces the Lord's Prayer in response to a direct request from Jesus' disciples. After observing Jesus in prayer, they ask him to teach them how to pray, much as John the Baptist had instructed his own followers. This context underscores the prayer's role as a practical tool for spiritual formation within the early Christian community.

When comparing the two versions, several notable differences emerge. Matthew's account is longer and more elaborate, including seven petitions compared to Luke's five. The Matthean version begins with "Our Father in heaven," while Luke's starts with the more concise "Father." Matthew includes the phrase "your will be done, on earth as it is in heaven," which is absent in Luke. Additionally, Matthew's version asks for "daily bread," while Luke uses the term "bread for each day."

These variations provide valuable insights into the early transmission and adaptation of Jesus' teachings. They suggest that the prayer was not transmitted as a fixed liturgical formula but rather as a flexible template that could be adapted to different contexts and needs. The differences may reflect the distinct theological emphases and pastoral concerns of the Matthean and Lukan communities.

One particularly significant addition to the Lord's Prayer is the doxology found in some manuscripts of Matthew's Gospel: "For the kingdom and the power and the glory are yours forever. Amen." This concluding praise is absent from the earliest and most reliable manuscripts and is not found in Luke's version. Scholars generally agree that it was a later addition, likely influenced by liturgical use in early Christian worship.

The presence of this doxology in later manuscripts illustrates the dynamic nature of the prayer's transmission and its ongoing development within Christian practice. It demonstrates how the Lord's Prayer, while rooted in Jesus' original teaching, continued to evolve and be shaped by the worshipping community.

The two Gospel accounts of the Lord's Prayer, with their similarities and differences, offer a window into the diverse ways early Christians understood and practiced Jesus' teachings on prayer. They reveal a living tradition that remained faithful to its core while adapting to new contexts and needs. This adaptability would prove crucial as the prayer spread beyond its Jewish-Christian origins to become a cornerstone of Christian worship and spirituality across diverse cultures and centuries.

Early Christian Use of the Lord's Prayer

The Lord's Prayer quickly became a cornerstone of early Christian practice, deeply embedded in the life and worship of the nascent church. As Christianity spread beyond its Jewish roots, this prayer served as a unifying force, providing a common spiritual language for diverse communities of believers.

Central to the catechetical process, the Lord's Prayer was one of the first texts taught to new converts. It served as a succinct summary of Christian faith and practice, encapsulating key theological concepts in a form that was easily memorized and recited. Church fathers like Tertullian and Cyprian wrote extensive commentaries on the prayer, unpacking its rich meanings for new believers and seasoned Christians alike.

The prayer also formed a foundation for early Christian liturgy. In many communities, it was recited at every gathering, often multiple times. Its inclusion in worship services helped to structure the liturgy and provided a familiar touchstone for congregants. The prayer's rhythmic cadence and poetic structure made it particularly suitable for communal recitation, fostering a sense of unity among worshippers.

Preparation for baptism often centered around the Lord's Prayer. Catechumens would spend weeks or even months studying and meditating on its words before being deemed ready for baptism. The prayer was seen as a gateway to full participation in the Christian community, with its recitation marking a significant milestone in a believer's spiritual journey.

Beyond formal worship settings, the Lord's Prayer played a crucial role in establishing daily prayer rhythms for early Christians. Following Jewish custom, many believers adopted the practice of praying at set times throughout the day. The Lord's Prayer, with its comprehensive scope and concise form, became a natural choice for these regular devotions. It provided a framework for personal prayer, guiding believers in their individual conversations with God.

Early church fathers devoted considerable attention to explicating the Lord's Prayer. Origen, Augustine, and John Chrysostom, among others, wrote extensive treatises exploring its depths. These commentaries not only helped to standardize interpretation but also demonstrated the prayer's centrality to Christian thought and practice. Through their exegesis, the church fathers drew out layers of meaning, connecting the prayer to broader theological concepts and ethical teachings.

The widespread use and study of the Lord's Prayer in these various contexts – catechism, liturgy, baptismal preparation, daily devotion, and theological reflection – underscores its fundamental importance in shaping early Christian identity and practice. It provided a common language of faith that transcended geographical and cultural boundaries, helping to forge a sense of unity among the diverse communities that made up the early church. As Christianity continued to spread and evolve, the Lord's Prayer remained a constant, anchoring believers in the teachings of Jesus and connecting them to the broader Christian tradition.

Theological Developments in Early Christianity

The Lord's Prayer served as a catalyst for significant theological developments in early Christianity, shaping the way believers understood core concepts of their faith. One of the most profound shifts was in the understanding of God as "Father." While the concept of God as a paternal figure existed in Judaism, Jesus' intimate use of "Abba" and the prayer's opening line, "Our Father," revolutionized the way Christians related to the divine. This familial language fostered a sense of intimacy and accessibility in the believer's relationship with God, while also emphasizing the communal nature of faith through the use of "our" rather than "my."

The concept of God's Kingdom, central to Jesus' teachings, found new expression in early Christian thought through the Lord's Prayer. The petition "Your kingdom come" became a focal point for eschatological expectations and ethical imperatives. Early Christians interpreted this not only as a future hope but also as a present reality to be manifested through their lives and communities. This dual understanding of the Kingdom as both "now" and "not yet" profoundly shaped Christian theology and practice.

The phrase "Give us this day our daily bread" sparked rich theological reflection on God's provision. While some interpreted it literally as a request for physical sustenance, others saw deeper spiritual significance. Origen, for instance, connected it to the Eucharist and the spiritual nourishment of God's word. This multifaceted interpretation reflected the early church's holistic view of salvation, encompassing both material and spiritual needs.

The prayer's emphasis on forgiveness became a cornerstone of early Christian theology. The reciprocal nature of forgiveness —"forgive us our debts, as we also have forgiven our debtors"—challenged believers to embody divine grace in their interpersonal relationships. This concept profoundly influenced the development of Christian ethics and the church's understanding of reconciliation, both with God and within the community.

Finally, the closing petitions about temptation and evil prompted early Christians to grapple with complex theological questions about the nature of sin, human free will, and God's role in human struggles. The phrase "lead us not into temptation" was particularly challenging, leading to various interpretations. Some, like Tertullian, understood it as a plea for God's protection against overwhelming trials, while others saw it as a request for strength to resist moral failings.

These theological developments, catalyzed by reflection on the Lord's Prayer, were not merely academic exercises. They deeply influenced the way early Christians understood their faith, shaped their worship practices, and guided their daily lives. The prayer became a lens through which believers interpreted their experiences and a framework for understanding their relationship with God and each other. As such, it played a crucial role in the formation of Christian doctrine and spirituality in the formative years of the church.

The Lord's Prayer in Early Christian Worship

The Lord's Prayer quickly became a cornerstone of early Christian worship, its influence permeating both communal gatherings and private devotions. As the early church grew and developed its distinct identity, this prayer, taught by Jesus himself, served as a unifying force and a powerful expression of Christian faith.

In communal worship settings, the Lord's Prayer took on a central role. Early Christian gatherings, often held in homes or secret locations due to persecution, incorporated the prayer as a regular part of their liturgy. It served as a collective affirmation of faith and a reminder of the core teachings of Jesus. The prayer's concise yet profound nature made it ideal for memorization and recitation, allowing even new converts to participate fully in worship.

Beyond communal settings, the Lord's Prayer also became an essential element of private devotion. Early Christians were encouraged to pray it multiple times daily, fostering a sense of constant communion with God. This practice helped to internalize the prayer's teachings and provided a structured framework for personal spiritual reflection. The prayer's emphasis on daily bread, forgiveness, and protection from temptation resonated deeply with the practical and spiritual needs of believers navigating a often hostile world.

As Christian communities grew and became more established, artistic representations of the Lord's Prayer began to emerge. These visual depictions, found in early catacomb paintings and later in more elaborate church frescoes and mosaics, served as powerful teaching tools in a largely illiterate society. They helped to reinforce the prayer's importance and aided in its memorization and contemplation.

The Lord's Prayer also found expression in early Christian music. While the exact melodies are lost to history, we know from various historical sources that the prayer was often chanted or sung as part of worship services. These musical settings not only enhanced the prayer's beauty but also aided in its memorization and emotional impact, allowing worshippers to engage with its words on a deeper level.

Perhaps most significantly, the Lord's Prayer played a crucial role in shaping Christian identity within the Roman world. In a time when Christians were often viewed with suspicion or outright hostility, the prayer served as a distinctive marker of faith. Its regular recitation reinforced the unique beliefs and values of the Christian community, setting them apart from both their Jewish roots and the surrounding pagan culture.

The prayer's emphasis on God as Father, the coming of His Kingdom, and the forgiveness of sins stood in stark contrast to the religious norms of the time. It reflected a radical new understanding of the relationship between humanity and the divine, one that would come to define Christianity as it spread throughout the Roman Empire and beyond.

Moreover, the Lord's Prayer acted as a unifying force among diverse Christian communities. Despite differences in language, culture, and specific theological interpretations, the shared practice of praying these words created a sense of unity and common purpose among believers scattered across the Roman world.

In essence, the integration of the Lord's Prayer into early Christian worship was not merely a liturgical development but a fundamental shaping force in the formation of Christian identity and practice. Its words, repeated daily in homes and gathering places across the empire, served as a constant reminder of the teachings of Jesus and the core values of the emerging faith, solidifying its place at the heart of Christian spirituality for generations to come.

From Jewish Roots to Christian Tradition

The Lord's Prayer stands as a remarkable testament to the seamless transition from Jewish religious practice to early Christian tradition. This prayer, taught by Jesus to his disciples, serves as a bridge between these two faiths, embodying both continuity and innovation in the nascent Christian movement.

The prayer's Jewish roots are undeniable, reflecting the spiritual landscape from which Christianity emerged. Its themes of God's kingdom, daily provision, and forgiveness echo throughout Jewish liturgy and scripture. However, the early Christian community imbued these familiar concepts with new meaning, filtered through the lens of Jesus' life, death, and resurrection.

As Christianity began to distinguish itself from Judaism, the Lord's Prayer played a crucial role in shaping a unique Christian identity. While maintaining reverence for Jewish tradition, early Christians used this prayer to express their distinct understanding of God as Father and their place in His divine plan. The prayer became a touchstone for Christian worship, setting it apart from other religious practices in the Roman world.

The influence of the Lord's Prayer extended far beyond its original text. It served as a template for the development of other Christian prayers and liturgical elements. Its concise yet profound structure inspired countless other invocations and supplications throughout Christian history. The themes encapsulated in this brief prayer became foundational to Christian theology, shaping discussions on God's nature, human dependence on divine provision, the concept of forgiveness, and the reality of spiritual warfare.

Perhaps most significantly, the Lord's Prayer acted as a unifying force among diverse early Christian communities. As the faith spread across geographical and cultural boundaries, this prayer provided a common language of devotion. From Jerusalem to Rome, from Syria to Egypt, early Christians could find common ground in these words, regardless of their background or specific theological leanings.

The journey of the Lord's Prayer from its Jewish roots to becoming a cornerstone of Christian tradition illustrates the complex and nuanced relationship between these two faiths. It reminds us that Christianity did not emerge in a vacuum, but rather grew organically from the rich soil of Jewish spirituality. At the same time, it demonstrates how early Christians, guided by their understanding of Jesus' teachings, were able to take familiar elements and transform them into something uniquely their own.

As we reflect on this transition, we see in the Lord's Prayer a microcosm of early Christian development – a faithful preservation of ancestral wisdom combined with bold reinterpretation in light of new revelation. This prayer, so deeply rooted in Jewish soil yet flourishing in Christian practice, continues to nourish the faith of millions, serving as a living link to the very foundations of Christian spirituality.

CHAPTER 9: HISTORICAL DEVELOPMENT: FROM EARLY CHURCH TO MODERN ERA

The Lord's Prayer in the Early Church (1st-3rd Centuries)

The Lord's Prayer, as taught by Jesus to his disciples, quickly became a cornerstone of early Christian practice and spirituality. In the first three centuries of the Church's existence, this profound invocation played a pivotal role in shaping the faith and practices of the nascent Christian community.

Central to the early Church's catechism, the Lord's Prayer served as a fundamental teaching tool for new converts. It encapsulated the essence of Christian theology and ethics in a concise, memorable form. Church leaders and teachers used the prayer as a framework to explain core Christian beliefs, helping neophytes understand concepts such as God's fatherhood, the coming of His kingdom, and the importance of forgiveness.

The prayer's integration into early Christian liturgy and worship was swift and comprehensive. It became a regular feature in communal gatherings, serving as both a unifying recitation and a structural element in worship services. The simplicity and depth of the prayer made it accessible to all believers, regardless of their background or level of education, fostering a sense of unity and shared purpose among the diverse early Christian communities.

Particularly significant was the role of the Lord's Prayer in baptismal preparation. Catechumens were required to learn and understand the prayer as part of their journey towards full initiation into the Christian faith. The prayer was often taught line by line, with each phrase unpacked to reveal its spiritual significance. This practice not only ensured that new Christians understood the prayer but also internalized its teachings as a guide for their new life in Christ.

As the early Church developed its rhythms of daily prayer, the Lord's Prayer emerged as a central element. Christians were encouraged to recite the prayer multiple times a day, following the Jewish tradition of fixed-hour prayer. This practice, advocated by early Church fathers like Tertullian and Origen, helped to structure the spiritual lives of believers and maintain a constant awareness of God's presence throughout their daily activities.

The theological richness of the Lord's Prayer did not go unnoticed by the early Church fathers. Luminaries such as Cyprian of Carthage, Origen, and Tertullian produced extensive commentaries on the prayer, exploring its depths and drawing out its implications for Christian life and doctrine. These early interpretations laid the groundwork for centuries of theological reflection on the prayer's meaning and significance.

Cyprian, in his treatise on the Lord's Prayer, emphasized its role in fostering unity among believers, writing, "Before all things, the Teacher of peace and Master of unity did not wish prayer to be made singly and individually, as for one who prays to pray for himself alone." This understanding of the prayer as a communal act, binding believers together in shared supplication, became a hallmark of early Christian thought.

As persecutions intensified in the second and third centuries, the Lord's Prayer took on additional significance as a source of strength and solidarity for the beleaguered Christian communities. Its petitions for daily bread and deliverance from evil resonated deeply with those facing hardship and threat, while its emphasis on forgiveness challenged believers to maintain Christ-like love even in the face of oppression.

By the end of the third century, the Lord's Prayer had become firmly established as a foundational text of Christian faith and practice. Its influence permeated every aspect of early Church life, from individual spiritual formation to communal worship and theological reflection. The prayer's journey from the lips of Jesus to the heart of early Christian spirituality set the stage for its continued impact throughout the subsequent centuries of Church history.

Medieval Period Developments (4th-15th Centuries)

The medieval period witnessed a significant evolution in the understanding, practice, and cultural integration of the Lord's Prayer. As Christianity became more established and spread across Europe, the prayer took on new dimensions in both religious and secular life.

Artistic representations of the Lord's Prayer flourished during this era, becoming a common theme in illuminated manuscripts. Skilled scribes and artists meticulously crafted intricate designs and illustrations surrounding the prayer text, often using gold leaf and vibrant pigments. These beautiful renditions not only served to elevate the prayer's status but also played a crucial role in religious education, particularly for the illiterate masses who could grasp the prayer's essence through visual storytelling.

Theological explorations of the Lord's Prayer reached new depths during the medieval period. Influential church fathers and scholars, such as Augustine of Hippo and Thomas Aquinas, penned extensive commentaries on the prayer, dissecting its every phrase and uncovering layers of meaning. These theological treatises sparked debates and discussions that would shape Christian thought for centuries to come. The prayer became a focal point for exploring broader theological concepts, including the nature of God, human free will, and the relationship between divine providence and human responsibility.

In the realm of popular devotion, the Lord's Prayer took on an increasingly central role in lay spirituality. As literacy rates remained low, the prayer's simplicity and profundity made it accessible to people from all walks of life. It became a cornerstone of personal piety, often recited multiple times daily as a form of spiritual discipline and protection. Laity would frequently use the prayer as a measuring stick for the passage of time, reciting it a set number of times for various daily tasks or as penance.

The medieval period also saw the Lord's Prayer set to music in various forms. Gregorian chants based on the prayer's text became an integral part of monastic life and liturgical worship. These haunting melodies not only enhanced the prayer's meditative quality but also aided in its memorization and transmission across linguistic boundaries. As polyphonic music developed in the later Middle Ages, more complex musical settings of the Lord's Prayer emerged, reflecting the prayer's elevated status in both ecclesiastical and cultural spheres.

Monastic traditions played a pivotal role in preserving and propagating the Lord's Prayer during this era. The prayer was incorporated into the Rule of St. Benedict and other monastic rules, ensuring its regular recitation throughout the day. Monasteries became centers of learning and spiritual practice, with monks and nuns dedicating significant time to contemplating and expounding upon the prayer's meanings. This monastic focus helped maintain the prayer's centrality in Christian life and contributed to its spiritual and intellectual development.

The medieval period thus marked a time of rich elaboration and deepening significance for the Lord's Prayer. From artistic beauty to theological profundity, from popular piety to monastic discipline, the prayer permeated nearly every aspect of medieval Christian culture. This era laid the groundwork for the prayer's enduring influence, setting the stage for the transformations and reinterpretations that would come with the dawn of the Reformation.

The Lord's Prayer During the Reformation Era (16th-17th Centuries)

The Reformation era marked a significant turning point in the history of Christianity, and the Lord's Prayer was not exempt from the sweeping changes that characterized this period. As Protestant reformers sought to return to what they perceived as the pure, biblical roots of the faith, the Lord's Prayer became a focal point for theological reexamination and practical application.

One of the most notable developments during this time was the emergence of Protestant-Catholic dialogues and debates centered on the Lord's Prayer. Reformers like Martin Luther and John Calvin, while maintaining the prayer's importance, challenged certain Catholic interpretations and practices associated with it. For instance, Luther criticized the use of the Lord's Prayer in what he saw as mechanical repetitions, emphasizing instead its role in personal, heartfelt communication with God.

The translation of the Lord's Prayer into vernacular languages was another crucial development of the Reformation era. As part of the broader movement to make scripture accessible to the common people, reformers translated the prayer into local languages. This had a profound impact on lay spirituality, allowing individuals to engage with the prayer in their native tongues and fostering a more personal connection with its words.

Theological reinterpretations of the Lord's Prayer by reformers were also significant. While maintaining its scriptural authority, Protestant thinkers often approached the prayer with fresh eyes, seeking to understand its meaning in light of their rediscovered emphasis on grace and faith. For example, Calvin's commentary on the Lord's Prayer stressed its role in shaping believers' understanding of God's sovereignty and human dependence on divine provision.

The Reformation era also saw a renewed emphasis on personal prayer and individual spirituality. The Lord's Prayer, previously often recited in Latin as part of formal church liturgies, became a cornerstone of Protestant private devotional practices. Reformers encouraged believers to use the prayer as a model for their own personal prayers, fostering a more intimate and individual approach to spiritual life.

Finally, the Lord's Prayer played a crucial role in emerging Protestant liturgies. As new forms of worship were developed, the prayer often retained a central place, albeit with different emphases. In many Protestant traditions, it became a unifying element, recited corporately as an expression of shared faith, rather than as a priestly invocation.

The Reformation era thus witnessed a transformation in how the Lord's Prayer was understood, translated, and practiced. While maintaining its scriptural authority and central importance, the prayer was reexamined and reapplied in ways that reflected the broader theological and ecclesiastical shifts of the time. This period set the stage for further developments in the prayer's interpretation and use in subsequent centuries, demonstrating its enduring relevance and adaptability across changing historical and cultural contexts.

Enlightenment and Modern Period (18th-20th Centuries)

The Enlightenment and Modern Period marked a significant shift in the perception and study of the Lord's Prayer. As rationalism and scientific inquiry took center stage, scholars began applying new methodologies to analyze this ancient text.

Scholarly analysis and historical-critical approaches gained prominence during this era. Researchers delved into the linguistic origins of the prayer, examining its Aramaic roots and comparing it with other Jewish prayers of the time. This academic scrutiny led to deeper insights into the prayer's historical context and original meaning, sometimes challenging traditional interpretations.

Despite the rise of secularism, the Lord's Prayer continued to serve as an ecumenical bridge between various Christian denominations. As the ecumenical movement gained momentum in the 20th century, the prayer became a unifying force, reminding different Christian traditions of their shared heritage. It was often used in interdenominational gatherings and joint worship services, symbolizing the common ground among diverse Christian groups.

The fields of psychology and sociology also turned their attention to the Lord's Prayer during this period. Researchers began studying the psychological impact of reciting the prayer, exploring its effects on mental well-being, stress reduction, and spiritual growth. Sociologists examined how the prayer functioned as a social binding agent within communities and its role in shaping collective religious identity.

As Christianity spread globally through missionary efforts,

the Lord's Prayer underwent numerous adaptations in various cultural contexts. Missionaries faced the challenge of translating the prayer into languages that lacked equivalent concepts for terms like "bread" or "kingdom." These efforts led to creative contextualizations that made the prayer more accessible and meaningful to diverse cultures while preserving its essential message.

The prayer also found a significant role in social justice movements of the 19th and 20th centuries. Activists and reformers often invoked the phrase "Thy kingdom come" as a rallying cry for social change, interpreting it as a call for justice and equality on earth. The prayer's emphasis on forgiveness and daily provision resonated with those fighting against oppression and poverty.

During World War I and II, the Lord's Prayer took on added significance for many soldiers and civilians alike. It provided comfort in times of extreme distress and served as a reminder of shared humanity amidst the horrors of war. Accounts from the trenches and bomb shelters often mentioned the recitation of the Lord's Prayer as a source of solace and unity.

The advent of mass media in the 20th century brought new visibility to the Lord's Prayer. Radio broadcasts of church services made the prayer accessible to those unable to attend in person. Later, television and film depictions of religious practices often featured the recitation of the Lord's Prayer, further cementing its place in popular culture.

Towards the end of the 20th century, as religious pluralism became more pronounced in many societies, the Lord's Prayer sometimes became a point of contention in public spaces. Debates arose over its recitation in schools and government functions, reflecting broader discussions about the role of religion in public life.

Throughout this period of rapid change and intellectual

ferment, the Lord's Prayer demonstrated remarkable resilience. It adapted to new contexts, withstood critical scrutiny, and continued to offer meaning and comfort to millions. The prayer's journey through the Enlightenment and Modern Period reflects its enduring power to speak to human needs and aspirations across time and cultural boundaries.

Contemporary Applications and Interpretations (Late 20th-21st Centuries)

As we enter the late 20th and early 21st centuries, the Lord's Prayer continues to evolve and find new relevance in our rapidly changing world. This ancient text has demonstrated a remarkable ability to adapt to contemporary contexts while maintaining its core spiritual essence.

In the realm of interfaith dialogue and comparative religious studies, the Lord's Prayer has become a focal point for exploring commonalities between different faith traditions. Scholars and religious leaders have engaged in fruitful discussions, comparing the themes and structure of the Lord's Prayer with similar invocations in other religions. These conversations have not only fostered greater understanding between faith communities but have also shed new light on the universal human yearning for connection with the divine.

The digital age has brought about new ways of engaging with the Lord's Prayer. Social media platforms and mobile applications now offer daily reminders and reflections on the prayer, making it accessible to millions at the touch of a button. Online communities have formed around shared recitations and discussions of the prayer, creating virtual spaces for spiritual connection and growth. This digital presence has allowed the Lord's Prayer to reach individuals who may not regularly attend traditional religious services, expanding its influence beyond the walls of churches and other places of worship.

Modern theological reinterpretations have breathed fresh life into the ancient words of the Lord's Prayer. Contemporary theologians and spiritual leaders have explored how the prayer speaks to current issues such as environmental stewardship, social justice, and personal well-being. For instance, the phrase "Give us this day our daily bread" has been reinterpreted to address issues of global hunger and sustainable food production. These new perspectives have helped to keep the prayer relevant and meaningful for modern believers grappling with complex global challenges.

In an unexpected development, the Lord's Prayer has found application in mental health and therapeutic settings. Psychologists and counselors have recognized the prayer's potential for promoting mindfulness, reducing anxiety, and fostering a sense of connection and purpose. Some therapists incorporate elements of the prayer into meditation exercises or use its themes as a framework for discussing personal growth and healing. This secular application of the prayer demonstrates its enduring psychological power, even outside of strictly religious contexts.

Perhaps most significantly, the Lord's Prayer continues to play a vital role in addressing contemporary social issues. Activists and community leaders often invoke the prayer's themes of forgiveness, justice, and divine guidance in their work for social change. The prayer has been recited at protests, vigils, and community gatherings, serving as a unifying force and a call to action. Its emphasis on collective well-being ("our Father," "give us," "forgive us") resonates strongly in an era marked by growing awareness of social interconnectedness and shared responsibility.

As we navigate the complexities of the 21st century, the Lord's Prayer remains a touchstone for millions, offering guidance, comfort, and inspiration. Its ability to speak to contemporary concerns while maintaining its timeless spiritual core is a testament to its enduring power and relevance. In a world often characterized by rapid change and uncertainty, the Lord's Prayer continues to provide a steady anchor, connecting present-day believers with a two-thousand-year tradition of faith and devotion.

Artistic and Cultural Influences Throughout History

The Lord's Prayer has left an indelible mark on the artistic and cultural landscape throughout history, inspiring countless creatives across various mediums. In literature, the prayer has been a recurring theme, with authors incorporating its words and concepts into their works. From Dante's "Divine Comedy" to T.S. Eliot's "The Waste Land," the prayer's influence can be traced through centuries of literary masterpieces. Contemporary writers continue to draw inspiration from its themes, often using the prayer as a metaphor for human longing, forgiveness, and the search for meaning.

Visual arts have provided a rich canvas for interpreting the Lord's Prayer. Medieval illuminated manuscripts adorned the prayer with intricate designs and gold leaf, elevating it to a work of art in itself. Renaissance painters like El Greco and Rembrandt created powerful depictions of Jesus teaching the prayer, while modern artists have offered abstract interpretations that capture its spiritual essence. The prayer's words have been etched into stained glass windows, carved into stone sculptures, and woven into tapestries, each piece offering a unique visual meditation on its meaning.

Music has perhaps been the most prolific medium for artistic expressions of the Lord's Prayer. Composers throughout history have set the prayer to music, resulting in a vast repertoire of choral works, hymns, and solo performances. From the Gregorian chants of the Middle Ages to Mozart's "Ave Verum Corpus" and contemporary gospel renditions, the prayer has been sung in countless languages and styles. These musical interpretations have not only enhanced worship experiences but have also brought the prayer's message to wider audiences through concerts and recordings.

The world of cinema and theater has also embraced the Lord's Prayer, often using it as a powerful dramatic device. In films, the recitation of the prayer has marked moments of intense emotion, spiritual awakening, or communal solidarity. Stage productions have incorporated the prayer in both religious and secular contexts, exploring its themes through drama, dance, and experimental theater. These performances have brought the prayer to life for audiences, inviting them to engage with its message in new and thought-provoking ways.

Perhaps one of the most pervasive cultural influences of the Lord's Prayer has been its impact on language itself. Phrases from the prayer have become idiomatic expressions in many languages, particularly in English. "Daily bread," "lead us not into temptation," and "thy will be done" are just a few examples of how the prayer's language has seeped into everyday speech, often used by people who may not even be aware of their origin. This linguistic influence underscores the prayer's deep cultural resonance and its ability to transcend religious boundaries.

The artistic and cultural expressions inspired by the Lord's Prayer serve as a testament to its enduring power and universal appeal. Through various art forms, the prayer has been continually reinterpreted and reimagined, allowing each generation to engage with its timeless wisdom in fresh and meaningful ways. As we reflect on this rich artistic legacy, we are reminded of the prayer's capacity to inspire, challenge, and move people across diverse cultures and historical periods, cementing its place not just in religious practice, but in the broader tapestry of human creative expression.

Challenges and Controversies in the Prayer's Historical Journey

Throughout its long history, the Lord's Prayer has not been without its share of challenges and controversies. These debates and disagreements have often reflected broader theological, cultural, and societal shifts, highlighting the prayer's central role in Christian thought and practice.

One persistent area of contention has been textual variations and translation debates. As the prayer spread across different languages and cultures, subtle differences in wording and interpretation emerged. The most notable example is the doxology "For thine is the kingdom, and the power, and the glory, forever. Amen." This phrase, absent in early manuscripts of Luke and disputed in Matthew, became standard in many Protestant traditions while remaining excluded from Catholic usage. Such variations have led to ongoing scholarly discussions about the prayer's original form and meaning.

Theological disagreements over interpretation have also marked the prayer's journey. Different Christian traditions have emphasized various aspects of the prayer, leading to diverse understandings of its petitions. For instance, the meaning of "daily bread" has been debated – does it refer to literal sustenance, spiritual nourishment, or both? Similarly, the nature of forgiveness as expressed in the prayer has been a point of theological reflection and sometimes disagreement.

The Lord's Prayer has not been immune to political uses and misuses throughout history. Rulers and regimes have at times co-opted the prayer's language to legitimize their authority or policies. During periods of religious conflict, such as the Reformation era, the prayer sometimes became a marker of confessional identity, with slight variations in its recitation used to distinguish between Catholic and Protestant adherents.

In more recent times, the prayer has faced challenges related to secularization and declining religious knowledge. As societies have become increasingly secular, particularly in the West, familiarity with the Lord's Prayer has diminished in some quarters. This trend has led to debates about the prayer's place in public life, such as its recitation in schools or government functions.

Contemporary challenges to the prayer's relevance and meaning have also emerged. Some critics argue that the prayer's language and concepts are outdated or difficult for modern individuals to relate to. Others have raised questions about the prayer's gender-exclusive language, leading to discussions about inclusive adaptations.

Despite these challenges, the Lord's Prayer has demonstrated remarkable resilience. Many believers and theologians have engaged with these controversies creatively, finding new ways to understand and apply the prayer's timeless wisdom. For instance, feminist theologians have offered fresh interpretations that emphasize God's nurturing qualities, while liberation theologians have highlighted the prayer's themes of justice and equality.

Moreover, these challenges have often spurred deeper reflection on the prayer's meaning and significance. Debates over translation and interpretation have led to richer understandings of the prayer's nuances and its roots in Jesus' teaching. Efforts to make the prayer relevant to contemporary concerns have resulted in thoughtful adaptations and reinterpretations that speak to modern spiritual needs.

In facing these challenges, the Lord's Prayer has continually demonstrated its capacity for renewal and reinterpretation. Far from diminishing its importance, these controversies have often served to underscore the prayer's enduring relevance and its ability to speak to diverse human experiences across time and culture. As such, the challenges faced by the Lord's Prayer throughout history stand as a testament to its profound impact and its continuing significance in the lives of believers and in broader cultural discourse.

CHAPTER 10: PSYCHOLOGICAL AND SOCIAL IMPACTS OF THE LORD'S PRAYER

Psychological Well-being and the Lord's Prayer

The Lord's Prayer, despite its ancient origins, continues to offer profound psychological benefits to those who engage with it regularly. This section explores how this timeless prayer addresses fundamental aspects of human psychology, providing a framework for mental and emotional well-being in our modern world.

At its core, the Lord's Prayer offers a powerful mechanism for processing guilt and fostering forgiveness. The line "forgive us our trespasses, as we forgive those who trespass against us" serves as a catalyst for psychological healing. By acknowledging our own shortcomings and extending forgiveness to others, individuals can release the burden of guilt and resentment that often weighs heavily on the psyche. For instance, a case study of individuals using the prayer to overcome guilt and shame revealed significant improvements in self-esteem and overall mental health. Participants reported feeling a sense of liberation and renewed self-worth after incorporating this aspect of the prayer into their daily practice.

The prayer also plays a crucial role in managing anxiety through the concept of surrender. By encouraging believers to submit their will to a higher power - "Thy will be done" - the prayer provides a psychological anchor in times of uncertainty. This act of surrender can significantly reduce anxiety by alleviating the pressure of feeling solely responsible for life's outcomes. Research findings on prayer and anxiety reduction have consistently shown that individuals who practice this form of spiritual surrender experience lower levels of stress and anxiety compared to those who don't.

Furthermore, the Lord's Prayer promotes a healthy perspective on material needs. The phrase "Give us this day our daily bread" encourages contentment with having one's basic needs met, rather than constantly striving for excess. This approach can significantly reduce stress related to materialism and consumerism, which are prevalent issues in our modern society. Testimonials from individuals practicing minimalism inspired by this aspect of the prayer often report increased life satisfaction and decreased anxiety about financial matters.

The communal aspect of the Lord's Prayer also fosters psychological well-being through social connection. The use of "Our Father" and "us" throughout the prayer emphasizes the importance of community and shared spiritual experiences. Studies on social bonding through group prayer practices have shown that participants experience increased feelings of belonging and social support, which are crucial factors in maintaining good mental health.

Lastly, regular recitation of the Lord's Prayer can build psychological resilience. The prayer's structure and content provide a stable framework for facing life's challenges. A long-term study on prayer practitioners and their ability to cope with life challenges revealed that those who regularly recited the Lord's Prayer demonstrated greater emotional stability and adaptability in the face of adversity. The prayer serves as a cognitive anchor, helping individuals maintain perspective and hope during difficult times.

In conclusion, the Lord's Prayer offers a multifaceted approach to psychological well-being. By addressing guilt, anxiety, materialism, social connection, and resilience, this ancient prayer continues to provide relevant and effective support for mental and emotional health in our contemporary world. Its enduring power lies in its ability to touch on fundamental human needs and experiences, offering a timeless remedy for the psychological challenges of any era.

Social Impact of the Lord's Prayer

The Lord's Prayer, despite its ancient origins, continues to exert a profound influence on modern society. Its impact extends far beyond individual spiritual practice, shaping social interactions, community values, and collective behaviors in numerous ways.

One of the most significant social impacts of the Lord's Prayer is its role in promoting forgiveness and reconciliation. The prayer's explicit call to "forgive us our trespasses, as we forgive those who trespass against us" serves as a powerful reminder of the importance of forgiveness in maintaining social harmony. This principle has inspired numerous community reconciliation programs worldwide. For instance, in post-apartheid South Africa, faith-based organizations have used the Lord's Prayer as a foundation for healing workshops, bringing together individuals from different racial backgrounds to work through historical grievances and build a more unified society.

The prayer also plays a crucial role in encouraging social responsibility. The opening words, "Our Father," immediately establish a sense of communal identity, reminding those who pray that they are part of a larger family. This perspective fosters a sense of collective welfare and mutual care. Many faith-based social initiatives draw inspiration from this aspect of the prayer. For example, the Catholic Worker Movement, founded by

Dorothy Day, bases its commitment to social justice and care for the poor on the principles embodied in the Lord's Prayer.

Another significant social impact is the prayer's ability to balance individual needs with communal welfare. While it acknowledges personal concerns ("Give us this day our daily bread"), it places these within the context of broader societal needs ("Thy kingdom come, Thy will be done"). This dual focus has influenced the structure and mission of many community organizations. The Salvation Army, for instance, models its approach on this balance, addressing immediate individual needs while also working towards broader societal transformation.

The Lord's Prayer has also proven instrumental in providing common ground across denominational divisions. As one of the few prayers shared by almost all Christian denominations, it serves as a unifying force in ecumenical movements and interfaith dialogue. Interfaith prayer gatherings often center around the Lord's Prayer, using it as a starting point for discussions on shared values and common spiritual aspirations. This has contributed to greater understanding and cooperation among different faith communities.

Moreover, the prayer has shown remarkable adaptability in addressing contemporary social issues. The concept of "Thy kingdom come" has been reinterpreted by many to encompass a wide range of social justice concerns. Environmental stewardship movements, for example, have drawn inspiration from this phrase, seeing care for the Earth as part of bringing about God's kingdom. Similarly, anti-poverty campaigns have used the prayer's emphasis on "daily bread" to advocate for more equitable distribution of resources.

The social impact of the Lord's Prayer is also evident in its influence on ethical decision-making in various sectors. Business leaders and healthcare professionals often turn to the prayer's principles when navigating complex moral dilemmas.

Its emphasis on forgiveness, justice, and communal welfare provides a framework for ethical considerations that extend beyond mere profit or efficiency.

Lastly, the prayer's impact on social cohesion cannot be overlooked. Regular communal recitation of the Lord's Prayer, whether in church services, school assemblies, or other gatherings, creates a shared experience that reinforces social bonds. This shared spiritual practice can foster a sense of unity and shared purpose within communities.

In conclusion, the Lord's Prayer continues to shape social dynamics in profound and multifaceted ways. From promoting forgiveness and reconciliation to encouraging social responsibility, from bridging denominational divides to addressing contemporary social issues, its influence permeates numerous aspects of societal life. As society continues to evolve, the prayer's timeless principles seem poised to remain a relevant force in shaping social interactions and collective values.

Personal Development Through the Lord's Prayer

The Lord's Prayer, despite its ancient origins, continues to serve as a powerful tool for personal growth and development in the modern world. This section explores how the prayer's principles can be applied to foster individual growth, emotional maturity, and spiritual well-being.

One of the key aspects of personal development facilitated by the Lord's Prayer is the cultivation of healthy dependency versus toxic independence. In a society that often glorifies self-reliance, the prayer reminds us of the importance of acknowledging our dependence on a higher power. This approach fosters a balanced perspective on autonomy and interdependence, encouraging individuals to seek support and guidance while still taking responsibility for their actions. Many personal growth programs have incorporated this aspect of the prayer, teaching participants how to navigate the delicate balance between self-sufficiency and openness to external support.

The Lord's Prayer also plays a significant role in building humility while maintaining dignity. The phrase "Thy will be done" encourages individuals to set aside their ego and align themselves with a greater purpose. However, this humility is not self-deprecating; rather, it's rooted in the understanding of one's place within a larger cosmic order. This concept has been particularly influential in leadership training, where the prayer serves as a model for humble leadership. Leaders who embody this principle often demonstrate greater empathy, better listening skills, and a more collaborative approach to decision-making.

Another crucial aspect of personal development addressed by the Lord's Prayer is the cultivation of a balanced approach to material needs. The phrase "Give us this day our daily bread" teaches contentment and responsible stewardship. It encourages individuals to focus on their present needs rather than excessive wants, promoting a healthier relationship with material possessions. This principle has been applied in various financial management courses, helping individuals develop a more mindful and sustainable approach to consumption and wealth management.

The Lord's Prayer also serves as a powerful tool for encouraging daily spiritual practice. Its brevity and depth make it an ideal centerpiece for consistent spiritual habits. Many individuals use the prayer as a framework for daily reflection, meditation, or journaling. In recent years, numerous apps and digital tools have been developed around the daily recitation of the Lord's Prayer, making it easier for people to integrate this practice into their busy modern lives.

Lastly, the Lord's Prayer cultivates mindfulness and present-moment awareness. The focus on "this day" in the prayer encourages individuals to ground themselves in the present, rather than dwelling on past regrets or future anxieties. This aspect of the prayer aligns well with contemporary mindfulness practices, and many meditation programs have incorporated elements of the Lord's Prayer into their techniques. By regularly reciting and reflecting on the prayer, individuals can develop greater emotional regulation, stress resilience, and overall well-being.

In conclusion, the Lord's Prayer offers a comprehensive framework for personal development that remains relevant in today's world. From fostering healthy dependency and humility to encouraging mindfulness and balanced materialism, the prayer provides timeless wisdom for individual growth. As we continue to navigate the complexities of modern life, the principles embedded in this ancient prayer offer valuable guidance for personal transformation and spiritual maturity.

Modern Applications in Various Contexts

The Lord's Prayer, despite its ancient origins, continues to offer profound guidance for navigating the complexities of modern life. This section explores how the timeless principles embedded in this prayer can be applied to address contemporary challenges across various contexts.

In our increasingly materialistic society, the Lord's Prayer serves as a powerful antidote to rampant consumerism. The prayer's emphasis on seeking "daily bread" rather than excess wealth encourages individuals to reassess their relationship with material possessions. This principle has inspired various anti-consumerism movements, promoting minimalism and conscious consumption. For instance, the "Buy Nothing" groups that have sprung up in communities worldwide often cite the prayer's teachings as a foundational philosophy, encouraging members to share resources and reduce unnecessary purchases.

The digital age has brought with it a unique set of anxieties, from social media addiction to information overload. The

Lord's Prayer offers a framework for addressing these modern stressors. Its call to "lead us not into temptation" can be interpreted as a guide for maintaining healthy boundaries with technology. Digital detox programs have begun incorporating elements of the prayer, using its principles to help participants cultivate mindfulness and reduce dependency on digital devices. One such program, "Disconnect to Reconnect," uses the prayer's structure to guide participants through a week-long technology fast, encouraging reflection on priorities and fostering real-world connections.

In the realm of work-life balance, the Lord's Prayer provides valuable perspective. Its holistic approach, addressing both spiritual and physical needs, offers guidance for those struggling to juggle career demands with personal well-being. Corporate wellness programs have started to recognize the value of this ancient wisdom. For example, a Fortune 500 company recently introduced a "Wholeness at Work" initiative, drawing inspiration from the prayer's balanced approach to life's various aspects. The program encourages employees to set boundaries, prioritize personal relationships, and engage in regular reflection, mirroring the prayer's emphasis on daily spiritual practice.

When it comes to navigating complex moral decisions, the Lord's Prayer offers an ethical framework that transcends specific religious doctrine. Its principles of forgiveness, avoiding temptation, and seeking a higher purpose can guide decision-making in various professional fields. In healthcare, for instance, some ethics committees have begun using a decision-making model loosely based on the prayer's structure. This model encourages healthcare professionals to consider not just immediate medical outcomes, but also broader implications for patient dignity, community impact, and long-term well-being.

Finally, the Lord's Prayer has found a new role in facilitating interfaith dialogue. As a text familiar to many Christian denominations and respected in other Abrahamic faiths, it serves as a bridge for discussions between different religious traditions. Interfaith peace initiatives have used the prayer as a starting point for exploring shared values and fostering mutual understanding. The "Common Ground" project, for example, brings together leaders from various faith backgrounds to explore the universal themes present in the Lord's Prayer, using these discussions as a foundation for collaborative community service projects.

In each of these modern applications, we see the enduring relevance of the Lord's Prayer. Its principles of humility, forgiveness, mindfulness, and community responsibility continue to offer valuable guidance in addressing the unique challenges of our time. As society evolves, this ancient prayer demonstrates a remarkable ability to adapt, providing a stable foundation of wisdom upon which we can build solutions to contemporary issues.

Universal Elements of the Lord's Prayer

The Lord's Prayer, despite its ancient origins, possesses a remarkable ability to transcend cultural and denominational boundaries. This universality is one of its most powerful attributes, allowing it to remain relevant and impactful across diverse societies and belief systems. The prayer's adaptability is evident in the countless cultural variations of its interpretation and application. From bustling urban centers to remote villages, people have found ways to make the prayer's message resonate with their unique circumstances and worldviews.

At its core, the Lord's Prayer addresses fundamental human needs and experiences that are common to all people, regardless of their background or beliefs. It touches on universal concerns such as the need for sustenance, forgiveness, guidance, and protection. Cross-cultural studies have consistently shown the prayer's relevance in diverse societies, highlighting its ability to speak to the human condition in a way that transcends geographical and cultural boundaries.

Perhaps one of the most remarkable aspects of the Lord's Prayer is its applicability to both religious and secular ethical frameworks. While rooted in Christian tradition, the principles espoused in the prayer – such as forgiveness, humility, and community care – align with many secular ethical systems. This has led to the adoption of ethical guidelines inspired by the prayer in various secular organizations, demonstrating its broad appeal and universal wisdom.

The Lord's Prayer provides a structured framework for spiritual expression while simultaneously allowing for personal adaptation. This flexibility enables individuals to tailor their interpretation and use of the prayer to their own spiritual journey. Creative adaptations of the prayer have emerged in various spiritual practices, ranging from contemplative meditations to artistic expressions, showcasing its versatility as a template for personal spiritual growth.

Despite the rapid pace of societal change, the Lord's Prayer continues to offer timeless wisdom that remains relevant in our modern world. Its enduring relevance is a testament to its ability to address core human needs and values that persist regardless of technological advancements or cultural shifts. Contemporary reinterpretations of the prayer have emerged to address modern challenges, such as environmental stewardship, digital overwhelm, and global interconnectedness, demonstrating its adaptability to new contexts.

The universal elements of the Lord's Prayer make it a powerful tool for fostering understanding and unity across diverse groups. Its ability to speak to shared human experiences creates common ground for dialogue and mutual respect. In an increasingly divided world, the prayer serves as a reminder of our shared humanity and the values that connect us all.

As we continue to navigate the complexities of modern life, the Lord's Prayer stands as a beacon of wisdom, offering guidance that is both ancient and ever-new. Its universal elements ensure that it will continue to resonate with people across cultures, providing a source of comfort, inspiration, and ethical direction for generations to come.

The Lord's Prayer in Therapeutic and Counseling Settings

The Lord's Prayer has found a unique and powerful application in modern therapeutic and counseling settings. Mental health professionals and spiritual counselors have recognized the prayer's potential to address deep-seated psychological issues and promote emotional healing.

In cognitive-behavioral therapy, the structure of the Lord's Prayer serves as a framework for challenging and reframing negative thought patterns. The phrase "forgive us our debts, as we forgive our debtors" becomes a powerful tool for addressing issues of guilt, shame, and resentment. Therapists guide clients to explore their own need for forgiveness and their capacity to forgive others, often leading to breakthroughs in interpersonal relationships and self-acceptance.

Mindfulness-based therapies have also incorporated elements of the Lord's Prayer. The concept of "daily bread" is used to foster present-moment awareness and gratitude for life's simple blessings. Clients are encouraged to focus on immediate needs rather than getting lost in anxieties about the future, aligning with mindfulness principles of staying grounded in the present.

In addiction recovery programs, the Lord's Prayer's emphasis on surrendering to a higher power resonates deeply with many participants. The line "lead us not into temptation, but deliver us from evil" provides a mantra for those struggling with addictive behaviors, offering both a plea for strength and an affirmation of divine protection.

Family therapists have found the communal aspect of the prayer—beginning with "Our Father"—useful in addressing family dynamics. It serves as a reminder of shared heritage and interconnectedness, often helping to heal rifts and foster a sense of unity within fractured family systems.

In grief counseling, the prayer's acknowledgment of God's kingdom—a realm beyond our earthly existence—offers comfort to those grappling with loss. It provides a spiritual perspective on death and separation, helping clients find meaning and hope in the face of profound sorrow.

Pastoral counselors frequently use the Lord's Prayer as a starting point for deeper spiritual exploration. Each line of the prayer can spark profound discussions about one's relationship with the divine, personal values, and life purpose. This often leads to a more integrated sense of self and a stronger spiritual foundation for facing life's challenges.

Even in secular counseling settings, the universal themes of the Lord's Prayer—such as seeking guidance, acknowledging personal limitations, and striving for moral behavior—provide valuable talking points for exploring clients' belief systems and ethical frameworks.

Group therapy sessions have successfully used communal recitation of the Lord's Prayer to foster a sense of unity and shared purpose among participants. This practice often breaks down barriers between individuals, creating a safe space for vulnerability and authentic sharing.

In stress management programs, the calming rhythm of the prayer serves as a form of meditation, helping to lower cortisol levels and promote relaxation. Clients are taught to use the prayer as a centering technique during times of high stress or anxiety.

It's important to note that the use of the Lord's Prayer in therapeutic settings is always done with sensitivity to clients' diverse religious and cultural backgrounds. For those who don't resonate with the Christian context, the principles underlying the prayer are often extracted and presented in more universal terms.

The effectiveness of incorporating the Lord's Prayer into therapeutic practices has been supported by numerous case studies and client testimonials. Many report a deeper sense of peace, improved coping skills, and a more robust spiritual life as a result of engaging with the prayer in a therapeutic context.

As mental health professionals continue to recognize the importance of spirituality in overall well-being, the Lord's Prayer stands out as a time-tested resource for promoting psychological health and emotional resilience. Its integration into various therapeutic modalities demonstrates the enduring relevance of this ancient spiritual practice in addressing the complex mental health challenges of the modern world.

The Lord's Prayer as a Tool for Global Unity and Peace

The Lord's Prayer, with its universal themes and widespread recognition, serves as a powerful instrument for fostering global unity and peace. In a world often divided by political, cultural, and religious differences, this ancient prayer offers common ground and shared values that transcend boundaries.

At its core, the Lord's Prayer emphasizes the concept of a shared spiritual parent, addressing "Our Father." This inclusive language promotes a sense of global family, encouraging individuals to view humanity as a collective rather than separate entities. By reinforcing this idea of interconnectedness, the prayer naturally cultivates empathy and compassion for others, regardless of their background or beliefs.

The prayer's focus on forgiveness is particularly relevant in the context of global peace. The line "forgive us our trespasses, as we forgive those who trespass against us" provides a framework for conflict resolution and reconciliation on both personal and international levels. It encourages individuals and nations to let go of grudges, seek understanding, and work towards healing relationships. This principle has been successfully applied in various peace-building initiatives worldwide, from post-conflict reconciliation efforts in Rwanda to interfaith dialogue programs in the Middle East.

Furthermore, the prayer's emphasis on "daily bread" and basic needs reminds us of our shared human experiences and vulnerabilities. This can inspire global efforts to address issues such as poverty, hunger, and inequality. Many international aid organizations have drawn inspiration from this aspect of the prayer, focusing on providing essential resources and support to communities in need, thus contributing to global stability and peace.

The concept of "Thy kingdom come, Thy will be done on earth as it is in heaven" encourages individuals to work towards creating a better world. This aspirational element of the prayer has motivated countless social justice movements and environmental initiatives. It provides a vision of a harmonious global society that transcends current realities, inspiring people to strive for positive change.

In the realm of diplomacy and international relations, the Lord's Prayer has been used as a starting point for interfaith dialogue and cross-cultural understanding. Its familiarity across various Christian denominations and its resonance with themes found in other religious traditions make it an excellent tool for building bridges between different communities. Interfaith prayer gatherings often include recitations of the Lord's Prayer alongside prayers from other traditions, symbolizing unity in diversity.

The prayer's call to resist temptation and evil also provides a universal ethical framework that can guide global decision-making. In international forums, principles derived from the Lord's Prayer have been invoked to advocate for ethical governance, responsible leadership, and the pursuit of the common good over narrow self-interests.

Moreover, the regular recitation of the Lord's Prayer in various languages across the globe creates a sense of synchronicity and shared spiritual practice. This simultaneous engagement in a common activity, despite geographical distances, reinforces the idea of a global community united in purpose and spirit.

In conclusion, the Lord's Prayer, far from being merely a religious text, serves as a powerful tool for promoting global unity and peace. Its emphasis on shared humanity, forgiveness, basic human needs, aspiration for a better world, and universal ethical principles provides a framework for addressing global challenges. As we continue to navigate an increasingly interconnected world, the timeless wisdom encapsulated in this prayer offers guidance and inspiration for building a more harmonious global society. The Lord's Prayer reminds us that despite our differences, we are all part of a larger human family, sharing common hopes, needs, and aspirations for a peaceful world.

CHAPTER 11: CONTEMPORARY RELEVANCE AND MODERN APPLICATIONS

Addressing Modern Anxieties and Concerns

I n our fast-paced, technology-driven world, the Lord's Prayer emerges as a surprising antidote to many of the anxieties and concerns that plague modern life. Far from being an outdated relic, this ancient prayer offers profound insights and practical guidance for navigating the complexities of contemporary existence.

One of the most pressing issues of our time is the sense of disconnection that pervades our hyper-connected digital age. While social media platforms promise to bring us closer together, many people report feeling more isolated than ever. The Lord's Prayer, with its opening address of "Our Father," immediately grounds us in a sense of genuine connection – not just with a divine presence, but with a global community of believers. This simple phrase reminds us that we are part of something larger than ourselves, countering the individualism that often leads to loneliness in our society.

The prayer also offers a powerful antidote to the rampant materialism and consumerism that characterize much of modern life. In a world where we are constantly bombarded with advertisements telling us we need more to be happy, the petition for "daily bread" is a radical call to contentment and trust. It shifts our focus from accumulating possessions to appreciating the essentials of life. Many individuals who have embraced this principle report finding a deep sense of peace and satisfaction that no amount of shopping or acquiring could provide.

In an era often described as morally relativistic, where traditional ethical frameworks are frequently challenged or dismissed, the Lord's Prayer provides a clear and unwavering moral compass. The phrase "Thy will be done" offers a foundation for ethical decision-making that transcends situational ethics or personal convenience. This becomes particularly relevant when facing complex modern dilemmas in areas such as bioethics or environmental stewardship. By aligning our will with a higher purpose, we find guidance in navigating these challenging waters.

The prayer also serves as a powerful tool for managing the stress and anxiety that seem endemic to modern life. In a world where we often feel pressured to control every aspect of our lives, the act of surrendering to a higher power – as modeled in the Lord's Prayer – can be profoundly liberating. Numerous studies have shown the positive impact of prayer and meditation on mental health, with many practitioners reporting reduced stress levels, improved emotional regulation, and a greater sense of overall well-being.

Finally, in an age where work-life balance seems increasingly elusive, the structure of the Lord's Prayer offers a model for a more holistic approach to daily life. Its balanced focus on spiritual, physical, and relational needs provides a template for ordering our priorities. Many professionals have found that integrating the prayer's principles into their daily routines helps them maintain a healthier perspective on work, relationships, and personal well-being.

In essence, the Lord's Prayer, despite its ancient origins, speaks directly to many of the core challenges of modern life. It offers a path to genuine connection in an age of digital isolation, contentment in a consumerist culture, ethical clarity in morally ambiguous times, peace amidst stress and anxiety, and balance in our often fragmented lives. As we grapple with the unique pressures of contemporary existence, this timeless prayer continues to provide relevant and transformative guidance.

The Lord's Prayer in Personal Development

The Lord's Prayer, despite its ancient origins, offers a profound framework for personal growth and development in the modern world. Its timeless principles address fundamental aspects of human nature and spirituality that remain relevant regardless of societal changes.

One of the most significant contributions of the Lord's Prayer to personal development is its model for building healthy dependency while avoiding toxic independence. In a culture that often glorifies self-reliance, the prayer's opening address, "Our Father," reminds us of our inherent connection to something greater than ourselves. This acknowledgment of dependence on a higher power provides a foundation for developing healthy relationships and a balanced sense of self. Psychological research has increasingly recognized the importance of secure attachment in personal well-being, and the prayer's model of reliance on God offers a spiritual framework that aligns with these findings. For many, this approach to spirituality provides a secure base from which to explore the world and face life's challenges.

The prayer also offers a unique perspective on cultivating humility while maintaining personal dignity. By addressing God as Father and acknowledging His will, the prayer encourages a posture of humility. However, this humility is balanced with the affirmation of human worth implied in the familial relationship with the divine. This delicate balance provides a model for personal growth that avoids both arrogance and self-deprecation. In leadership contexts, this principle has been particularly influential, inspiring a style of servant leadership that combines confidence with a deep sense of responsibility and care for others.

Another crucial aspect of personal development addressed by the Lord's Prayer is the cultivation of a balanced approach to material needs. The petition for "daily bread" teaches contentment and responsible stewardship, offering a counterpoint to the consumerist mindset prevalent in modern society. This principle has inspired various approaches to financial planning and resource management that prioritize sufficiency over excess. Many individuals have found that aligning their material expectations with this model leads to greater satisfaction and reduced stress around financial matters.

The structure of the Lord's Prayer also provides a template for developing consistent spiritual practice. Its brevity and comprehensiveness make it an ideal tool for daily reflection and meditation. Many people have found that incorporating the prayer into their daily routines, whether through traditional recitation or more personalized adaptations, helps to center their thoughts and establish a regular connection with their spiritual beliefs. This consistency in spiritual engagement often translates into greater emotional stability and a clearer sense of purpose in daily life.

Perhaps one of the most powerful elements of the Lord's Prayer for personal development is its emphasis on forgiveness. The prayer's explicit linking of receiving forgiveness with extending it to others provides a profound model for emotional healing and interpersonal relationships. Psychological research has consistently shown the benefits of forgiveness for mental health, including reduced stress, anxiety, and depression. Therapeutic approaches that incorporate forgiveness practices inspired by the prayer have shown particular promise in addressing deep-seated emotional wounds and improving overall well-being.

In conclusion, the Lord's Prayer offers a multifaceted approach to personal development that addresses key aspects of emotional, spiritual, and relational growth. Its principles of healthy dependence, balanced humility, material contentment, consistent spiritual practice, and forgiveness provide a comprehensive framework for navigating the complexities of modern life. As individuals engage with these timeless truths, many find that the ancient words of the prayer continue to offer fresh insights and transformative power for personal growth in the contemporary world.

Social and Communal Impact

The Lord's Prayer, despite its ancient origins, continues to exert a profound influence on modern society and community dynamics. Its teachings offer valuable insights into fostering social cohesion, promoting reconciliation, and addressing contemporary societal challenges.

One of the most powerful aspects of the Lord's Prayer in terms of social impact is its emphasis on forgiveness and reconciliation. In a world often marked by division and conflict, the prayer's call to "forgive us our debts, as we forgive our debtors" provides a transformative model for breaking cycles of retaliation and resentment. This principle has found practical application in various post-conflict societies, where prayer-inspired approaches have been instrumental in healing deep-seated wounds.

For instance, in post-apartheid South Africa, the Truth and Reconciliation Commission drew inspiration from Christian principles of forgiveness, including those embodied in the Lord's Prayer. This process, while not without its critics, played a crucial role in the country's transition to democracy. Similarly, in Northern Ireland, interfaith prayer groups that included recitations of the Lord's Prayer served as neutral grounds for dialogue between Protestant and Catholic communities, contributing to the peace process.

The prayer's opening words, "Our Father," emphasize a communal focus that encourages social responsibility. This collective approach to addressing the divine reminds us that we are part of a larger human family, with shared responsibilities and destinies. This concept has inspired numerous community initiatives worldwide. For example, faith-based organizations have established community gardens, food banks, and homeless shelters, embodying the spirit of collective welfare inherent in the prayer.

The Lord's Prayer also provides a model for balancing individual needs with communal welfare. The petition for "daily bread" acknowledges personal needs, while the broader context of the prayer places these needs within a framework of collective well-being. This balance is reflected in social policies in various countries, particularly in Nordic nations known for their strong social safety nets combined with personal responsibility.

In an era of increasing secularization and religious diversity, the Lord's Prayer has emerged as a powerful tool for providing common ground across denominational divisions. Its universal themes and widespread familiarity make it an ideal starting point for ecumenical and even interfaith dialogue. Numerous interfaith initiatives have used the Lord's Prayer as a springboard for discussions about shared values and spiritual practices across different religious traditions.

The prayer's reference to "daily bread" has also informed contemporary discussions on economic justice and wealth distribution. Faith-based organizations addressing economic inequality often draw inspiration from this concept, interpreting it as a call for ensuring that all members of society have access to basic necessities. This has led to initiatives ranging from microfinance programs in developing countries to advocacy for living wage policies in wealthy nations.

However, it's important to acknowledge that the application of the Lord's Prayer to social issues is not without challenges. Critics argue that its Christian origins may limit its relevance in pluralistic societies. Others warn against oversimplifying complex social problems by reducing them to spiritual solutions alone.

Despite these challenges, the enduring impact of the Lord's Prayer on social and communal life is undeniable. Its principles of forgiveness, communal responsibility, and economic justice continue to shape social initiatives, policy discussions, and community-building efforts around the world. In a global society grappling with division, inequality, and conflict, the timeless wisdom encapsulated in this ancient prayer offers valuable insights for fostering more cohesive, compassionate, and just communities.

As we navigate the complexities of modern social challenges, the Lord's Prayer serves as a reminder of our shared humanity and our collective responsibility to care for one another. Its teachings continue to inspire individuals and communities to work towards a more just, peaceful, and harmonious world.

Psychological Well-being and the Lord's Prayer

The Lord's Prayer, despite its ancient origins, offers profound insights into psychological well-being that resonate deeply with contemporary understanding of mental health. This section explores how the prayer's components can contribute to emotional healing, stress reduction, and overall psychological resilience.

One of the most powerful psychological benefits of the Lord's Prayer lies in its approach to guilt and shame. The concept of divine forgiveness, encapsulated in the phrase "forgive us our debts," provides a powerful framework for processing these difficult emotions. Believing in unconditional divine forgiveness can be transformative, allowing individuals to release the burden of past mistakes and move forward with a renewed sense of self. This aspect of the prayer has been incorporated into various therapeutic approaches, particularly in faith-based counseling. Therapists have found that individuals who internalize this message of forgiveness often experience significant reductions in symptoms of depression and anxiety related to unresolved guilt.

The prayer's emphasis on surrendering to divine will, expressed in "Thy will be done," offers a unique perspective on managing anxiety. In a world where the illusion of control often leads to heightened stress, the act of "letting go" in the context of faith can provide immense psychological relief. This principle aligns closely with mindfulness practices, which emphasize acceptance of present circumstances. Many mental health professionals have developed mindfulness exercises inspired by this aspect of the prayer, helping individuals cultivate a sense of peace amidst life's uncertainties.

The concept of "daily bread" in the Lord's Prayer provides a fascinating lens through which to examine our relationship with material possessions and consumption. In today's consumer-driven society, the prayer's emphasis on sufficiency rather than excess offers a refreshing counterpoint to the relentless pursuit of more. Studies have consistently shown a negative correlation between materialism and life satisfaction. By reframing needs and wants through the perspective of "daily bread," individuals often report greater contentment and reduced anxiety related to financial matters.

The communal aspect of the Lord's Prayer, evident in its use of

"Our Father" rather than "My Father," speaks to the fundamental human need for connection. The psychological benefits of belonging to a praying community are well-documented. Research on social support and mental health in religious communities consistently shows that individuals who feel part of a spiritual collective tend to have lower rates of depression and anxiety. The shared experience of reciting the Lord's Prayer can foster a sense of unity and mutual support that extends beyond the moment of prayer itself.

Perhaps one of the most significant psychological benefits of engaging with the Lord's Prayer is the development of resilience. The prayer's underlying message of trust in divine provision can serve as a powerful coping mechanism in times of adversity. Numerous case studies have documented individuals who, through their faith and the principles embodied in the Lord's Prayer, have demonstrated remarkable resilience in the face of life's challenges. This trust in a higher power often translates into increased optimism and a greater capacity to navigate difficult circumstances.

It's important to note that the psychological benefits of the Lord's Prayer are not limited to those with religious beliefs. Even from a secular perspective, the principles embodied in the prayer - forgiveness, acceptance, gratitude, community, and resilience - align closely with many evidence-based practices in psychology. The prayer offers a structured way to engage with these concepts, providing a daily reminder of these important psychological principles.

In conclusion, the Lord's Prayer offers a rich resource for psychological well-being that transcends its religious origins. Its emphasis on forgiveness, surrender, contentment, community, and resilience provides a holistic approach to mental health that complements modern psychological understanding. As we continue to grapple with the complexities of mental health in the 21st century, the timeless wisdom encapsulated in this ancient prayer continues to offer valuable insights and practical strategies for cultivating psychological well-being.

The Lord's Prayer in Contemporary Spiritual Practice

The Lord's Prayer, despite its ancient origins, continues to play a vital role in contemporary spiritual practice across various denominations and even in interfaith contexts. Its enduring relevance is evident in the myriad ways it is incorporated into modern spiritual life, offering a timeless framework for connecting with the divine and navigating life's challenges.

One of the most powerful applications of the Lord's Prayer in contemporary practice is its use as a meditation focus. In an age where mindfulness and meditation have gained widespread popularity, the prayer offers a structured yet profound basis for contemplative practice. Practitioners often use each line of the prayer as a focal point, allowing the words to center their thoughts and guide their meditation. For instance, meditating on "Our Father, who art in heaven" can evoke a sense of divine presence and cosmic perspective, while "Give us this day our daily bread" might prompt reflection on gratitude and trust in divine provision. Guided meditation techniques based on the Lord's Prayer have been developed by spiritual directors and mindfulness experts, offering a bridge between traditional Christian practice and contemporary wellness approaches.

In the realm of interfaith dialogue, the Lord's Prayer serves as a valuable starting point for discussions with other faith traditions. Its themes of divine reverence, forgiveness, and spiritual sustenance find echoes in many world religions, providing common ground for meaningful interfaith conversations. Interfaith events often feature shared exploration of prayer traditions, with the Lord's Prayer offering a familiar yet profound text for collective reflection. These dialogues not only foster mutual understanding but also highlight the universal human yearning for connection with the divine, transcending doctrinal differences.

For many individuals, the Lord's Prayer serves as a template for personal prayer, informing and structuring their private devotional life. Its comprehensive nature, addressing both spiritual and material needs, provides a model for balanced and holistic prayer. Many believers use the prayer's structure as a framework, expanding on each line to address personal concerns and aspirations. For example, the line "Thy kingdom come" might prompt prayers for social justice and personal spiritual growth, while "Forgive us our trespasses" could lead to specific acts of confession and reconciliation.

In communal worship, the Lord's Prayer continues to play a central role across diverse Christian traditions, serving as a unifying element in ecumenical gatherings. Its near-universal recognition among Christians makes it a powerful tool for fostering unity amidst denominational diversity. Ecumenical services often feature the Lord's Prayer as a centerpiece, with participants joining in this shared heritage regardless of their specific doctrinal backgrounds. This practice not only reinforces the prayer's status as a cornerstone of Christian faith but also serves as a reminder of the fundamental unity underlying various Christian expressions.

Finally, the Lord's Prayer has found renewed importance as a tool for spiritual self-examination. Each line of the prayer can serve as a prompt for deep personal reflection and spiritual inventory. Retreat programs and spiritual formation courses often use the prayer as a structural element, encouraging participants to engage deeply with each phrase and examine their lives in light of its teachings. For instance, reflecting on "Lead us not into temptation" might prompt an examination of personal weaknesses and strategies for spiritual resilience, while "Thy will be done" could inspire contemplation on surrender and alignment with divine purposes.

In all these contemporary applications, the Lord's Prayer demonstrates its remarkable adaptability and enduring relevance. It continues to offer guidance, comfort, and inspiration to modern spiritual seekers, proving that ancient wisdom can speak powerfully to contemporary needs. As a bridge between tradition and innovation, the personal and the communal, and the spiritual and the practical, the Lord's Prayer remains a vital resource in the landscape of contemporary spirituality.

The Lord's Prayer and Contemporary Social Issues

The Lord's Prayer, despite its ancient origins, provides a powerful framework for addressing some of the most pressing social issues of our time. Its timeless principles offer guidance and inspiration for tackling complex challenges in our modern world.

Environmental stewardship is a critical concern in our era of climate change and ecological degradation. The phrase "Thy will be done on earth" takes on new significance when viewed through an environmental lens. It suggests that humanity's role is not to exploit the earth, but to align our actions with divine intent for creation. This perspective has inspired numerous faith-based environmental initiatives. For instance, the "Green Church" movement encourages congregations to reduce their carbon footprint, promote sustainable practices, and advocate for environmental policies. These efforts demonstrate how the prayer's principles can motivate concrete action for planetary well-being.

In the realm of conflict resolution, the Lord's Prayer offers a radical model of forgiveness and reconciliation. In a world often locked in cycles of retaliation and vengeance, the prayer's emphasis on forgiving others "as we are forgiven" provides a path towards breaking these destructive patterns.

This approach has been adopted in various peacemaking efforts worldwide. The Truth and Reconciliation Commission in post-apartheid South Africa, while not explicitly based on the prayer, embodied its spirit of forgiveness and healing. Similarly, conflict resolution workshops in war-torn regions often incorporate principles of mutual forgiveness and shared humanity that echo the prayer's teachings.

The digital age presents unprecedented ethical challenges, and here too, the Lord's Prayer offers relevant guidance. The concept of "lead us not into temptation" takes on new meaning in the context of online behavior. It encourages users to be mindful of the digital temptations that can lead to harmful actions like cyberbullying, spreading misinformation, or engaging in online harassment. Some faith-based organizations have developed social media guidelines inspired by the prayer's principles, promoting responsible digital citizenship and online ethics.

Mental health support is another area where the Lord's Prayer has found contemporary application. The prayer's themes of trust, forgiveness, and surrender can be powerful tools in mental health treatment. Many therapists and counselors, particularly those working within faith-based frameworks, incorporate elements of the prayer into their practice. For example, the concept of surrendering to a higher power, as expressed in "Thy will be done," is often used in addiction recovery programs. The prayer's emphasis on forgiveness can also be a valuable resource in addressing issues of guilt, shame, and relational healing.

Lastly, the Lord's Prayer offers a model for community building in increasingly fragmented societies. The opening words, "Our Father," immediately establish a sense of shared identity and common humanity. This communal aspect has inspired neighborhood initiatives aimed at fostering social cohesion. Community dinners, shared prayer gatherings, and local service projects organized around the prayer's themes of mutual care and shared responsibility have helped build bridges across social, economic, and cultural divides.

In each of these areas - environmental stewardship, conflict resolution, digital ethics, mental health support, and community building - the Lord's Prayer demonstrates its enduring relevance. Its principles, far from being outdated, offer profound insights into addressing contemporary social issues. By reinterpreting and applying these ancient words to modern contexts, individuals and communities continue to find guidance, inspiration, and practical solutions for the challenges of our time. The prayer's ability to speak to such diverse and pressing concerns underscores its universal and timeless nature, proving that spiritual wisdom can indeed offer valuable perspectives on even the most complex social issues of the 21st century.

Critiques and Challenges

While the Lord's Prayer has maintained its significance for centuries, it has not been immune to criticism and challenges in the modern era. This section explores various perspectives that question or critique the prayer's relevance and application in contemporary society.

One of the most prominent critiques comes from secularist viewpoints, which argue that the prayer's religious nature makes it irrelevant in an increasingly secular world. Secularists contend that moral and ethical guidance can be derived from non-religious sources, rendering the Lord's Prayer unnecessary for personal or societal development. This perspective is often voiced in debates about the role of religion in public life, such as the controversy surrounding the recitation of the Lord's Prayer in schools or government institutions.

Feminist theologians and scholars have raised concerns about the gendered language in the prayer, particularly the use of "Our Father." They argue that this masculine imagery reinforces patriarchal structures and may alienate those who relate to the divine in feminine or non-gendered terms. In response, some communities have adopted alternative versions of the prayer, using gender-neutral language or incorporating feminine imagery. For instance, some progressive Christian communities use phrases like "Our Creator" or "Our Mother and Father in heaven" to address these concerns while maintaining the prayer's core meaning.

Postcolonial critiques examine the Lord's Prayer through the lens of cultural imperialism. Critics argue that the prayer's widespread use, particularly in areas colonized by Western Christian powers, has sometimes come at the expense of indigenous spiritual practices. This perspective challenges the universal application of the prayer and calls for greater recognition of diverse cultural and spiritual traditions. In response, some indigenous Christian communities have developed contextualized versions of the Lord's Prayer that incorporate local language, imagery, and cultural concepts while preserving the prayer's essential elements.

The efficacy of prayer itself has been questioned from a scientific standpoint. Skeptics argue that the effects of prayer cannot be empirically measured or verified, challenging the notion that prayer can influence real-world outcomes. This critique extends to the Lord's Prayer, questioning whether its recitation can truly lead to the fulfillment of its petitions. While some studies have attempted to measure the effects of prayer on health outcomes, results have been inconclusive, leading to ongoing debates about the intersection of faith and science.

Finally, there's a concern about maintaining the depth and sanctity of the Lord's Prayer in popular culture. As the prayer has become deeply ingrained in Western culture, it has sometimes been used in ways that some consider trivializing or commercializing. For example, the use of the prayer or its phrases in advertising, popular music, or as casual expressions has led to debates about whether such usage diminishes its spiritual significance. Some argue that these cultural references keep the prayer relevant, while others contend that they risk reducing a profound spiritual tool to a mere cultural artifact.

These critiques and challenges do not negate the Lord's Prayer's importance for millions of believers worldwide. Instead, they invite deeper reflection on its meaning and application in a diverse, rapidly changing world. They challenge believers to engage thoughtfully with the prayer, considering its context, language, and implications in light of contemporary understandings and diverse perspectives. Ultimately, these critiques contribute to a richer, more nuanced appreciation of the Lord's Prayer, encouraging believers to engage with it not just as a rote recitation, but as a living, evolving spiritual resource that continues to inspire reflection, debate, and spiritual growth in the modern world.

CHAPTER 12: THE TIMELESS RESONANCE OF THE LORD'S PRAYER: A REFLECTION ON ITS ENDURING POWER AND UNIVERSALITY

The Timeless Wisdom of the Lord's Prayer

T he Lord's Prayer, despite its brevity, encapsulates a profound wisdom that has resonated across centuries and cultures. Its enduring power lies in its ability to address universal human needs, balance spiritual and material concerns, foster both individual and communal spirituality, offer simplicity alongside depth, and adapt across diverse cultural and denominational contexts.

At its core, the Lord's Prayer speaks to fundamental human experiences that transcend time and place. The prayer addresses our deepest longings for connection, provision, guidance, and forgiveness. When we pray "Give us this day our daily bread," we express a universal need for sustenance, both physical and spiritual. This plea resonates with people from all walks of life, whether in ancient agrarian societies or modern urban landscapes. Similarly, the petition for forgiveness - "Forgive us our debts, as we also have forgiven our debtors" - touches on the universal human experience of moral failing and the need for reconciliation.

One of the prayer's most remarkable features is its delicate balance between spiritual aspirations and earthly needs. It begins with lofty, cosmic appeals - "Hallowed be thy name, thy kingdom come, thy will be done" - before seamlessly transitioning to practical, everyday concerns. This harmonization of the divine and the mundane reflects the holistic nature of human existence, acknowledging that our spiritual lives are intrinsically linked to our physical realities. It reminds us that the sacred can be found in the ordinary, and that our daily lives are infused with spiritual significance.

The Lord's Prayer also uniquely nurtures both personal faith and communal spirituality. It begins with "Our Father," not "My Father," immediately placing the individual within the context of a larger community of faith. Yet, it still allows for deeply personal engagement with the Divine. This dual focus encourages believers to see their individual spiritual journey as part of a broader tapestry of faith, fostering a sense of connection and shared purpose.

Perhaps one of the most remarkable aspects of the Lord's Prayer is its combination of simplicity and depth. Its words are straightforward enough for a child to memorize, yet its concepts are so profound that theologians have spent lifetimes unpacking their meanings. This accessibility, coupled with its capacity for deep reflection, allows the prayer to meet individuals wherever they are on their spiritual journey. A young person might find comfort in the simple request for daily bread, while a seasoned spiritual seeker might contemplate the cosmic implications of

God's kingdom coming to earth.

Finally, the Lord's Prayer demonstrates an extraordinary adaptability across cultures and denominations. While deeply rooted in the Christian tradition, its themes of divine providence, forgiveness, and spiritual guidance resonate beyond denominational boundaries. It has been translated into countless languages, incorporated into diverse liturgical traditions, and even found appreciation among non-Christian spiritual seekers. This universality speaks to the prayer's ability to touch on fundamental aspects of the human spiritual experience.

In essence, the timeless wisdom of the Lord's Prayer lies in its capacity to speak to the core of human spirituality while remaining relevant across changing times and diverse cultures. It offers a spiritual framework that is at once deeply personal and universally applicable, simple yet profound, addressing both our highest aspirations and our most basic needs. As we continue to grapple with the complexities of modern life, the Lord's Prayer stands as a testament to the enduring power of spiritual wisdom, offering guidance, comfort, and challenge to all who engage with its words.

The Lord's Prayer in Contemporary Context

In our rapidly changing world, the Lord's Prayer continues to offer profound guidance and comfort, addressing the unique challenges and anxieties of modern life. This ancient prayer, rooted in timeless wisdom, proves remarkably adept at speaking to the concerns of our contemporary society.

One of the most striking ways the Lord's Prayer addresses modern anxieties is through its emphasis on surrender and trust. In a world characterized by constant change, information overload, and increasing uncertainty, the simple phrase "Thy will be done" offers a powerful antidote to stress and worry. By encouraging us to relinquish control and trust in a higher purpose, the prayer provides a calm center amidst the storm of modern life. It reminds us that despite the complexities of our world, there is a greater plan at work, offering solace to those overwhelmed by the pace of change or the weight of responsibility.

The prayer also serves as a potent counter to the rampant materialism and consumerism that define much of modern culture. In a society that often equates worth with wealth and success with accumulation, the humble request "Give us this day our daily bread" stands as a radical alternative. It shifts our focus from endless want to gratitude for sufficiency, challenging the "more is better" mentality that drives much of our economic anxiety. This simple phrase encourages contentment and mindfulness, inviting us to appreciate what we have rather than constantly striving for more. In doing so, it offers a path to greater peace and satisfaction in a world that often leaves us feeling inadequate or unfulfilled.

Perhaps one of the most relevant aspects of the Lord's Prayer for our times is its emphasis on forgiveness. In an era marked by deep social and political divisions, where grudges are nursed on social media and polarization seems to increase daily, the prayer's call to forgive "as we forgive those who trespass against us" is both challenging and essential. This teaching pushes us beyond our comfort zones, asking us to extend grace even to those we perceive as enemies. In practice, this could mean reaching across political divides, seeking reconciliation in fractured communities, or letting go of personal resentments. The prayer reminds us that forgiveness is not just a personal act but a social necessity, vital for healing our divided world.

Amidst the fluidity and rapid changes of modern life, the Lord's Prayer offers a sense of stability and continuity. Its use in both personal daily practice and formal liturgy provides an anchor of tradition in a sea of constant innovation. For many, the familiar words of the prayer, unchanged over centuries, offer comfort and a sense of connection to generations past. This continuity can be particularly meaningful in a time when many traditional institutions and practices are being questioned or abandoned. The prayer stands as a bridge between past and present, offering timeless wisdom in contemporary settings.

Finally, the Lord's Prayer serves as a unique bridge between the sacred and the secular in our increasingly diverse society. While deeply rooted in Christian tradition, many of its principles – such as forgiveness, community responsibility, and ethical living – resonate beyond religious boundaries. In secular contexts, the prayer's teachings can be applied as universal ethical principles, promoting compassion, social responsibility, and personal integrity. This ability to speak across the religious-secular divide makes the Lord's Prayer a valuable resource for building common ground in pluralistic societies.

In conclusion, the Lord's Prayer demonstrates a remarkable capacity to address the complexities and challenges of modern life. From offering peace in a stressful world to challenging materialism, from promoting forgiveness in divided times to providing stability amidst change, this ancient prayer continues to offer relevant and transformative wisdom. Its enduring power lies in its ability to speak to the core of human experience, transcending time and culture to address the deepest needs of the human heart, even in our fast-paced, ever-changing world.

The Psychological and Social Impact of the Lord's Prayer

The Lord's Prayer, despite its brevity, carries profound psychological and social implications that extend far beyond its religious context. This ancient prayer has demonstrated a remarkable ability to foster mental well-being, build community, provide ethical guidance, encourage personal growth, and promote social responsibility.

At its core, the Lord's Prayer serves as a powerful tool for promoting psychological well-being. By inviting individuals to surrender their concerns to a higher power, the prayer offers a sense of relief from the burdens of daily life. The act of acknowledging a divine presence and seeking guidance can significantly alleviate anxiety and depression. For many, the simple act of reciting "Thy will be done" provides a comforting reminder that they are not alone in facing life's challenges. This surrender to a higher purpose can lead to increased resilience and a more positive outlook on life.

The communal aspect of the Lord's Prayer plays a crucial role in building social cohesion. The use of plural pronouns throughout the prayer - "our," "us," "we" - emphasizes a collective identity that transcends individual concerns. This shared experience of prayer can bring diverse groups together, fostering a sense of unity and shared purpose. In times of crisis or celebration, the familiar words of the Lord's Prayer often serve as a rallying point, providing comfort and solidarity. Churches, schools, and even secular organizations have used the prayer as a means of bringing people together, reinforcing the bonds of community.

Beyond its community-building aspects, the Lord's Prayer offers a comprehensive framework for ethical living. Each phrase of the prayer can be interpreted as a guide for moral decision-making. For instance, "Thy will be done" encourages individuals to consider a higher purpose or greater good when faced with difficult choices. The prayer's emphasis on forgiveness - both receiving and extending it - provides a powerful model for conflict resolution and personal growth. In professional settings, the principles embedded in the Lord's Prayer can inform ethical business practices and leadership styles.

The Lord's Prayer also serves as an excellent tool for self-reflection and personal growth. Its concise yet profound statements invite deep introspection. Many individuals use the prayer as a daily self-examination exercise, reflecting on how well they've lived up to its ideals. Have they honored the divine in their actions? Have they been forgiving? Have they avoided temptation? This regular self-assessment can lead to significant personal development and character growth over time.

Lastly, the communal focus of the Lord's Prayer naturally extends to a broader sense of social responsibility. The petition "Thy kingdom come" has inspired countless initiatives aimed at addressing societal issues and creating a more just world. From soup kitchens to global charity organizations, many social outreach programs find their philosophical underpinnings in the principles of the Lord's Prayer. The prayer's emphasis on collective well-being encourages individuals to look beyond their personal needs and consider how they can contribute to the greater good of society.

In conclusion, the psychological and social impact of the Lord's Prayer is far-reaching and multifaceted. It provides a framework for mental health, community building, ethical living, personal growth, and social engagement. As such, it continues to be a relevant and powerful force in shaping both individual lives and broader social structures, demonstrating that its wisdom extends far beyond the bounds of religious practice into the realms of psychology and sociology.

The Lord's Prayer in Interfaith Dialogue

The Lord's Prayer, despite its distinctly Christian origins, has shown remarkable potential as a bridge for interfaith dialogue and understanding. Its universal themes and profound simplicity make it an excellent starting point for conversations across different faith traditions.

One of the most striking aspects of the Lord's Prayer in interfaith contexts is its ability to find common ground. Many religions share concepts of divine providence, the importance of daily sustenance, and the need for forgiveness. For instance, the idea of God as a provider resonates with Islamic teachings about Allah's benevolence, while the emphasis on forgiveness finds parallels in Buddhist principles of compassion and letting go. These shared concepts can serve as a foundation for meaningful interfaith discussions, allowing people of different faiths to recognize their common spiritual heritage.

However, the prayer also presents an opportunity to respectfully explore and understand differences. The concept of God as Father, central to the Lord's Prayer, can be a launching point for discussing various perspectives on the divine across different religions. While some faiths may not personify the divine in this way, the conversation can lead to a deeper understanding of how different traditions conceptualize and relate to the transcendent. This respectful exploration of differences can foster mutual understanding and appreciation for the diversity of human spiritual expression.

The Lord's Prayer's emphasis on widely shared ethical principles makes it particularly valuable in promoting universal values. The call for forgiveness, the acknowledgment of human fallibility, and the aspiration for a better world are themes that resonate across religious boundaries. Interfaith discussions centered on these aspects of the prayer can highlight the common ethical ground shared by different faith traditions, potentially leading to collaborative efforts in addressing social issues or promoting peace.

For many non-Christians, engaging with the Lord's Prayer can be a catalyst for deeper spiritual exploration. The prayer's structure and concepts often inspire reflection on one's own beliefs and practices. A Muslim participant in an interfaith dialogue might find the prayer's emphasis on daily bread reminiscent of the importance of gratitude in Islamic teachings. A Hindu might draw parallels between the prayer's acknowledgment of divine will and the concept of dharma. These connections can lead to rich conversations and a broader appreciation for diverse spiritual paths.

Perhaps most importantly, the Lord's Prayer has the potential to build bridges across traditions. Interfaith events or projects centered around shared values expressed in the prayer can bring communities together in powerful ways. For example, an interfaith initiative focused on forgiveness, inspired by the prayer's emphasis on this theme, could involve multiple religious communities working together to promote reconciliation in areas of conflict. Such collaborations not only foster understanding but also demonstrate the positive impact that interfaith cooperation can have on society.

In conclusion, while the Lord's Prayer is undoubtedly a Christian text, its wisdom and universality make it a valuable tool in interfaith dialogue. By serving as a starting point for finding common ground, respecting differences, promoting universal values, encouraging spiritual exploration, and building bridges across traditions, the prayer continues to demonstrate its relevance beyond the boundaries of Christianity. In our increasingly interconnected and diverse world, the Lord's Prayer stands as a testament to the potential for ancient wisdom to foster modern understanding and cooperation across faith traditions.

The Future of the Lord's Prayer

As we look ahead, the Lord's Prayer stands poised to continue its profound impact on spiritual life, adapting to new contexts while maintaining its timeless essence. The future of this ancient prayer is likely to be characterized by evolving interpretations, technological integration, responses to emerging global challenges, ongoing scholarly exploration, and a renewed emphasis on spiritual formation.

The interpretation and application of the Lord's Prayer will undoubtedly continue to evolve as each new generation brings fresh perspectives to its timeless words. Contemporary scholars and theologians are already uncovering new layers of meaning, informed by advances in linguistics, archaeology, and historical research. For instance, recent studies on first-century Aramaic are shedding new light on Jesus' original wording, potentially deepening our understanding of phrases like "daily bread" or "thy kingdom come."

In our increasingly digital world, the Lord's Prayer is finding new expressions through technology. We're seeing the emergence of prayer apps that offer daily reminders and reflections on each line of the prayer. Virtual reality experiences are being developed to create immersive environments for meditation on the prayer's themes. These technological adaptations are making the prayer more accessible to younger generations and those accustomed to digital forms of spirituality.

As we face unprecedented global challenges, the Lord's Prayer is likely to be reinterpreted in light of these new realities. For example, in the context of climate change and food insecurity, "Give us this day our daily bread" may take on new significance, prompting reflections on sustainable living and equitable resource distribution. The phrase "Thy kingdom come" might inspire renewed efforts for social justice and environmental stewardship.

Scholarly interest in the Lord's Prayer shows no signs of waning. Ongoing academic exploration promises to uncover more about the prayer's historical context, its place in early Christian worship, and its theological implications. Interdisciplinary studies, combining insights from theology, psychology, sociology, and neuroscience, may offer new perspectives on the prayer's impact on individual and communal well-being.

Looking forward, we may see a renewed emphasis on the Lord's Prayer in Christian education and spiritual formation. Recognizing the prayer's power to encapsulate core Christian beliefs and practices, churches and spiritual leaders might develop innovative curriculum and retreat programs centered around its teachings. These could range from in-depth studies for adults to creative, interactive programs for children and youth, all aimed at deepening engagement with this foundational text.

The future may also bring increased interfaith dialogue around the Lord's Prayer. As global communities become more interconnected, the prayer could serve as a bridge for understanding between different faith traditions, highlighting shared values while respectfully acknowledging differences.

In an era of rapid change and increasing secularization, the Lord's Prayer may take on new significance as an anchor of spiritual tradition. Its concise yet profound expression of human needs and divine relationship could appeal to those seeking spiritual depth without complex dogma.

As we envision the future of the Lord's Prayer, we can anticipate both continuity and innovation. Its core message will likely remain a powerful source of comfort, guidance, and challenge for believers, while its expression and application may evolve to meet the needs of each new age. Whether whispered in private devotion, chanted in grand cathedrals, or contemplated through digital platforms, the Lord's Prayer seems destined to continue its role as a central pillar of Christian spirituality, adapting to new contexts while preserving its timeless wisdom.

A Call to Continued Engagement

As we conclude our exploration of the Lord's Prayer, it becomes clear that this timeless invocation is not merely a historical artifact or a ritualistic recitation, but a living, breathing spiritual practice with profound relevance for our contemporary world. This final section serves as a clarion call for continued engagement with the Lord's Prayer, inviting readers to deepen their personal practice, strengthen their communities, and contribute to the ongoing scholarly and interfaith dialogue surrounding this remarkable prayer.

First and foremost, we extend an invitation to personal practice. The Lord's Prayer is not meant to be confined to the pages of this book or the walls of a church; it is a daily companion, a guide for navigating the complexities of modern life. We encourage readers to incorporate the prayer into their daily routines, whether through traditional recitation, contemplative meditation, or creative reinterpretation. Consider starting your day with the Lord's Prayer, allowing its words to set the tone for the hours ahead. Alternatively, you might choose to end your day with this prayer, reflecting on how its principles have manifested in your experiences. For those seeking a more immersive experience, consider a prayer journal, where you can explore each phrase of the Lord's Prayer in depth, relating it to your personal circumstances and spiritual journey.

Beyond individual practice, the Lord's Prayer offers a powerful framework for community application. Local faith communities, civic organizations, and even secular groups can draw inspiration from the prayer's principles to strengthen social bonds and address pressing issues. Consider organizing community service projects that embody the spirit of "Thy kingdom come," working to create a more just and compassionate society. Food banks inspired by "Give us this day our daily bread" or reconciliation initiatives echoing "Forgive us our debts, as we forgive our debtors" are just a few examples of how the Lord's Prayer can catalyze positive community action.

For those inclined towards academic and theological exploration, the Lord's Prayer remains a rich field for further study. We encourage scholars, theologians, and curious laypeople alike to continue delving into the linguistic, historical, and theological aspects of the prayer. Potential areas for investigation include comparative analyses of the prayer's use across different Christian traditions, explorations of its relevance to contemporary ethical dilemmas, or studies on its psychological impact on practitioners. The interdisciplinary nature of Lord's Prayer studies offers exciting opportunities for collaboration between theologians, historians, psychologists, sociologists, and scholars from other fields.

In our increasingly interconnected world, the Lord's Prayer can serve as a valuable tool for interfaith engagement. We urge readers to initiate or participate in interfaith dialogues centered on this prayer, exploring commonalities and respectfully discussing differences with people of other faith traditions. Interfaith prayer gatherings, panel discussions, or collaborative community service projects inspired by the Lord's Prayer can foster understanding and cooperation across religious boundaries. These encounters not only enrich our understanding of our own faith but also contribute to building a more harmonious, pluralistic society.

Finally, we invite readers to consider the global impact of continued engagement with the Lord's Prayer. In a world facing unprecedented challenges – from climate change to political polarization – the prayer's emphasis on divine guidance, collective responsibility, and forgiveness offers a moral compass for navigating complex issues. International peace initiatives, global environmental stewardship programs, or worldwide movements for social justice could all find inspiration and direction in the principles of the Lord's Prayer.

As we stand at the threshold of an uncertain future, the Lord's Prayer remains a beacon of hope, a call to faith, and a guide for action. Its words, simple yet profound, continue to resonate across cultures, generations, and belief systems. By engaging deeply with this prayer – in our personal lives, our communities, our academic pursuits, our interfaith dialogues, and our global endeavors – we participate in a living tradition that stretches back two millennia and forward into a future full of possibility.

Let us, then, approach the Lord's Prayer not as a static text, but as a dynamic invitation to spiritual growth, community engagement, and global transformation. May these ancient words continue to inspire, challenge, and guide us, echoing through our lives and our world as a testament to the enduring power of faith, hope, and love.

ABOUT THE AUTHOR

Daniel Hall

Daniel Hall is a USA TODAY and Wall Street Journal bestselling author who approaches faith and spirituality with the same practical mindset he brings to his other endeavors. Though not a theologian by training, Daniel's diverse background— including law, nursing, speaking, and entrepreneurship—has given him a unique perspective on how ancient wisdom can be applied to modern life.

Like the Lord's Prayer itself, Daniel believes spiritual insights don't need to be complex to be profound. His approach to this timeless prayer reflects his belief that the deepest truths are often expressed in the simplest words.

As the host of the top-rated Real Fast Results podcast, Daniel Hall YouTube channel and creator of numerous "Real Fast" training programs, Daniel has spent years helping people cut through complexity to find practical solutions. In this book, he applies this same accessible approach to spiritual growth, showing how the Lord's Prayer offers wisdom we can immediately apply to our daily lives.

Daniel's journey with the Lord's Prayer began not in seminary halls but in moments of personal challenge and growth. His interest springs not from academic study but from seeing firsthand how these 65 words have provided guidance, comfort, and clarity in both ordinary and extraordinary circumstances.

When not writing or speaking, Daniel can often be found sharing his insights as an enrichment speaker for Celebrity Cruise Lines' "Beyond the Podium" program and Royal Caribbean Cruise Lines' enrichment program. He has shared stages with luminaries such as Brian Tracy, Mark Victor Hansen, and many others at events across the country.

Daniel holds a JD from Texas Tech University and a BSN from the University of Texas at El Paso. He lives with a firm belief that spiritual wisdom, like the Lord's Prayer, is not meant to be locked away in scholarly tomes but lived out in the everyday moments that make up our lives.

www.ingramcontent.com/pod-product-compliance
Lightning Source LLC
LaVergne TN
LVHW051308080426
835509LV00020B/3161